FRANKENSTEIN

Mary Shelley

AUTHORED by Lucas Duclos
UPDATED AND REVISED by Ellie Campisano

COVER DESIGN by Table XI Partners LLC
COVER PHOTO by Olivia Verma and © 2005 GradeSaver, LLC

BOOK DESIGN by Table XI Partners LLC

Published by GradeSaver LLC, www.gradesaver.com

First published in the United States of America by GradeSaver LLC. 2016

GRADESAVER, the GradeSaver logo and the phrase "Getting you the grade since 1999" are registered trademarks of GradeSaver, LLC

ISBN 978-1-60259-659-7

Printed in the United States of America

For other products and additional information please visit http://www.gradesaver.com

Table of Contents

Biography of Mary Shelley (1797–1851)

It was apparent that the life of Mary Wollstonecraft Godwin was going to be out of step with the ordinary from the moment of her birth on August 30, 1797. She had both unorthodox parents and an orthodox family structure: her father, William Godwin, was a celebrated philosopher and historian who had briefly been a Calvinist minister. A cold, remote man who overate grossly and borrowed money from anyone who would give him a loan, he had little time for anything but his philosophical endeavors. This intellectual single-mindedness was somewhat modulated by his passion for Mary Wollstonecraft. With the possible exception of William Blake, Wollstonecraft was the most influential of the Enlightenment radicals. Having declared herself independent at the age of twenty-one, she ran a school with her sisters and was the respected friend of the philosopher Samuel Johnson. While in France, she had an affair with an army captain, which ended in the birth of her first daughter, Fanny. After the soldier abandoned her and the child, she returned to England and attempted suicide. Happily or unhappily, she failed, and began writing in a variety of genres. It was her revolutionary feminist writings, however, that won her lasting fame.

The first meeting between Godwin and Wollstonecraft took place at a dinner party at Godwin's home. Drawn to each other by virtue of their shared philosophical beliefs, the two began an affair begun in the autumn of 1796. When Mary discovered that she was pregnant, the couple decided to marry in order to legitimate both of Mary's children. The couple, however, in adherence to their enlightened views, continued to live and work independently. The pair remained devoted to each other, and Godwin was devastated when Wollstonecraft died shortly after the birth of their daughter, Mary. Although he was fond of his daughters, the task of raising them alone proved too much for Godwin, and he immediately set about finding a second wife. His proposal to Maria Reveley, who would later become Mary's best friend, was rejected.

He later married Mary Jane Clairmont, the first woman to respond to his overtures. This second wife proved to be a cruel, shallow woman who neglected Fanny and Mary in favor of her own children. Mary (who was so lively that her father had nicknamed her Mercury) was frequently whipped for impertinence; rebellion came naturally to the headstrong Mary, and she refused to be subdued. Though the girls were given lessons in domesticity (cooking, cleaning, and other wifely duties) Mary could not feign interest in such pursuits: she would simply take up a book and let the dinner burn. Her father was the most important person in her life, and his favor meant everything to her. She excelled in her lessons and could hold her own in adult conversation often with the great minds of her time from a remarkably early age. Around the age of eight, she began reading the writings of her mother. By the time she was ten, she had memorized every word of them.

Mary spent hours at her mother's grave, reading or eating meals when the atmosphere at home was particularly bad. This habit continued well into her teens, when she was sent to live at Ramsgate with a Miss Petman. This move was prompted by Mary's frailty and inability to concentrate at home. From Ramsgate, she journeyed to Scotland to stay with Baxter, a close friend of her father's. Living with the Baxters was the happiest time that Mary had thereto known. When she returned to London a year later, she had grown into a woman. She became closer to her father than ever before, and the two engaged in constant philosophical debate. This served, predictably, to augment her stepmother's hatred.

The poet Percy Shelley, a devoted follower and friend of William Godwin's, began spending a great deal of time in the Godwin home. Although he was married, his presence made an immediate impression on Mary, who began to read poetry at his inducement. Shelley's genuine admiration for the works of Mary's mother earned him her trust she invited him to accompany her on her visits to her mother's grave, and the two became inseparable. Their intellectual kinship was passionately felt by both of them, and they rapidly fell in love. Godwin was furious at this development, and immediately barred the poet from his home. The couple, however, refused to be separated and began a clandestine correspondence. With the help of Mary's stepsister, they were able to elope.

Setting up housekeeping in London was expensive, and money was very tight for the newly married pair. Relations between them were somewhat strained: Shelley's first wife Harriet belatedly bore him a son, and his good friend Thomas Hogg became enamored of Mary. To make matters worse, Mary became pregnant; the child, a daughter, died shortly after birth. Mary fell into an acute depression.

Having conceived a dislike for London (perhaps as a result of their misfortunes), the couple began traveling: in the English countryside, in France, and elsewhere. Mary was writing profusely, and published *Frankenstein* in 1818. No one could have predicted the extent of the book's popularity: it would remain the most widely read English novel for three decades. Although it was maliciously rumored that Percy Shelley was the book's true author, Mary was catapulted to the forefront of the struggle for recognition then being waged by woman writers.

Tragically, Percy Shelley drowned in a shipwreck in 1822. Though Mary was devastated, she remained dedicated to her son, Percy Florence. She spent the remainder of her life championing her husband's neglected poetry, and was eventually successful in forcing its publication. Mary Wollstonecraft Shelley died in her sleep at age fifty-four.

Teacher Guide - About the Author

Born August 30, 1797, Mary Shelley was the daughter of feminist philosopher Mary Wollstonecraft and cultural critic William Godwin. The second of two daughters to Wollstonecraft (the elder being Fanny Imlay from an engagement prior to William Godwin), Mary did not get to know her mother as Wollstonecraft died weeks later due to complications from her youngest daughter's birth.

In 1801, Godwin remarried to Mary Jane Clairmont, who had two children of her own: Clara and Charles. Godwin home-schooled Mary. He tailored his teachings to encompass a wide variety of fields, granting Mary access to his own personal library in the process. Godwin encouraged Mary's own writing. In 1808, he published her first works in the Godwin Juvenile Library. Along with this encouragement, he allowed for her to sit in on his intellectual meetings.

In 1812, at the age of 15, Mary was introduced to Godwin's admirer, Percy Shelley, at a dinner party. At the time Shelley was still married to his wife, Harriet. In 1812-1814, Mary spent time intermittently with friends away from home, supposedly due to problems with Mary Clairmont. Upon her return in July of 1814, Mary Godwin and Percy Shelley eloped to France. Later, Shelley's father cut his allowance, while William Godwin expressed his rage and feelings of betrayal. Mary and Percy began to move about the country with friends hoping to avoid their creditors. Mary gave birth to daughter Clara on Feb. 22, 1815. The child subsequently died on March 6 of the same year. Late in the year, Mary and Percy settled down in Bishop's Gate, where they spent their time in intense study.

Mary gave birth to son, William, on Jan. 24 of the next year. Percy, Mary, and her half-sister Clara then spent the summer in Geneva in search of Lord Byron (Clara believed him to be the father of her unborn child). It is here where they met up with Byron (who fled England in scandal after his wife walked out on him) at Villa Diodati on the shores of Lake Lamon. During their time summering, however, the weather was terrible, and they spent most of their hours indoors. It was during these many hours that Byron suggested a contest of "ghost stories" concerning the "nature of the principle of life" and its discovery.

It was here Mary conceived of Dr. Frankenstein and wrote a short story concerning him and his trials. With the support of Percy Shelley, she expanded the story into a novel. The novel was published anonymously in 1818. The dedication to her father, William Godwin, sparked initial criticism and interest. Due to the book's popularity, Mary Shelley placed her name as author on the second French edition. Mary eventually redrafted parts of the novel with Percy Shelley for the 1831 edition to modernize the work.

Teacher Guide - Study Objectives

If all of the elements of this lesson plan are employed, students will develop the following powers, skills, and understanding:

1. Students will be able to analyze the structure of the text, referring to the significance of first-person narration to the theme.

2. Students will be able to analyze language and tone, considering the author's writing style and the narrator's point of view.

3. Students will demonstrate how literary devices and elements may be combined to perform a close reading of the text.

4. Students will be able to use textual evidence to support interpretations and analyses of symbols, motifs, and themes.

5. Students will be able to use terms found within the text to strengthen vocabulary.

6. Students will be able to make informed observations about the historical context of the novel.

7. Students will be able to identify common tropes, rhetorical devices, and thematic content within the novel that can be used to develop arguments about information presented in the text.

Teacher Guide - Common Core Standards

1. 11-12

   CCSS.ELA-Literacy.CCRA.R.1 Read closely to determine what the text says explicitly and to make logical inferences from it; cite specific textual evidence when writing or speaking to support conclusions drawn from the text.

2. 11-12

   CCSS.ELA-Literacy.CCRA.R.2 Determine central ideas or themes of a text and analyze their development; summarize the key supporting details and ideas.

3. 11-12

   CCSS.ELA-Literacy.CCRA.R.3 Analyze how and why individuals, events, or ideas develop and interact over the course of a text.

4. 11-12

   CCSS.ELA-Literacy.CCRA.R.5 Analyze the structure of texts, including how specific sentences, paragraphs, and larger portions of the text (e.g., a section, chapter, scene, or stanza) relate to each other and the whole.

5. 11-12

   CCSS.ELA-Literacy.CCRA.R.6 Assess how point of view or purpose shapes the content and style of a text.

6. 11-12

   CCSS.ELA-Literacy.CCRA.R.7 Integrate and evaluate content presented in diverse media and formats, including visually and quantitatively, as well as in words.

7. 11-12

   CCSS.ELA-LITERACY.CCRA.R.8 Delineate and evaluate the argument and specific claims in a text, including the validity of the reasoning as well as the relevance and sufficiency of the evidence.

8. 11-12

CCSS.ELA-Literacy.CCRA.R.9 Analyze how two or more texts address similar themes or topics in order to build knowledge or to compare the approaches the authors take.

9. 11-12

CCSS.ELA-Literacy.CCRA.R.10 Read and comprehend complex literary and informational texts independently and proficiently.

10. 11-12

CCSS.ELA-Literacy.CCRA.W.2 Write informative/explanatory texts to examine and convey complex ideas and information clearly and accurately through the effective selection, organization, and analysis of content.

11. 11-12

CCSS.ELA-Literacy.CCRA.W.3 Write narratives to develop real or imagined experiences or events using effective technique, well-chosen details and well-structured event sequences.

12. 11-12

CCSS.ELA-Literacy.CCRA.W.6 Use technology, including the Internet, to produce and publish writing and to interact and collaborate with others.

13. 11-12

CCSS.ELA-Literacy.CCRA.W.7 Conduct short as well as more sustained research projects based on focused questions, demonstrating understanding of the subject under investigation.

14. 11-12

CCSS.ELA-Literacy.CCRA.W.8 Gather relevant information from multiple print and digital sources, assess the credibility and accuracy of each source, and integrate the information while avoiding plagiarism.

15. 11-12

CCSS.ELA-Literacy.CCRA.SL.1 Prepare for and participate effectively in a range of conversations and collaborations with diverse partners, building on others' ideas and expressing their own clearly and persuasively.

16. 11-12

CCSS.ELA-Literacy.CCRA.SL.4 Present information, findings, and supporting evidence such that listeners can follow the line of reasoning and the organization, development, and style are appropriate to task, purpose, and audience.

17. 11-12

   CCSS.ELA-Literacy.CCRA.SL.5 Make strategic use of digital media and visual displays of data to express information and enhance understanding of presentations.

18. 11-12

   CCSS.ELA-Literacy.CCRA.SL.6 Adapt speech to a variety of contexts and communicative tasks, demonstrating command of formal English when indicated or appropriate.

19. 11-12

   CCSS.ELA-Literacy.CCRA.L.5 Demonstrate understanding of figurative language, word relationships, and nuances in word meanings.

Teacher Guide - Introduction to Frankenstein

A success in its own right, *Frankenstein* stands out as an even greater triumph because of the unlikeliness of such an accomplishment by a female novelist at the time. The early nineteenth century was not an easy time to be a female writer, never mind a novelist. Though her novel is regularly classified a gothic-style or horror story, and is often looked at as one of the first of its kind, her contemporaries regarded it as a novel about ideas. More specifically, it did well to promote some of William Godwin's philosophy, nevertheless standing in explicit opposition to the idea that humans can achieve perfection, and it remains a testament to the ruin that can come of such an idea.

Shelley's *Frankenstein* is an example of the Gothic movement in literature — a form that was only just becoming popular in England at the time of its publication. The movement was a reaction against the humanistic, rationalist literature of The Age of Reason. One might say it was ushered in by the death of Keats, the English author with whom Romanticism is perhaps most closely associated. *Frankenstein* might be seen as a compromise between the Gothic approach and the Romantic one in that it addresses serious philosophical subjects in a fantastical manner. It confronts the human condition, but it can hardly be said to take place in a natural world recognizable to the everyday person.

The first edition of the novel was published anonymously. Despite this, the novel's unprecedented success paved the way for some of the most prominent female writers of the nineteenth century, including George Eliot, George Sand and the Bronte sisters. All of them owed Mary a tremendous literary debt. Without this text, many female authors might never have endeavored to write; and they might never have felt as free to express philosophical material.

Key Aspects of Frankenstein

Tone

There are several narrators in the story, and the tone shifts slightly across the transitions between them. Each narrator tells his story to only one individual, and this makes the tone very personal. Even with these changing narrators, there is a sense of impending doom hanging over each of their narratives. Walton's letters are intimate and take the tone of a sibling, discussing desires, doubts, fears and fascinations. Frankenstein's takes on a grave, tone, and reads more like a cautionary, haunted tale. The creature's narrative takes on the tone of a dark memoir.

Setting

While the setting changes with the shift in narrator and tense, the narrative that
frames them all (Walton's) is set inside his ship, which is stuck in the ice in the north.
So whether the events of any given narrative occur in Victor's home in Geneva, the
laboratory at Ingolstadt or in the Orkney islands of Scotland, a cottage in Germany or
a villa on lake Como in Italy, the mood of the entire story is set by this framing
narrative's setting. The closed-in cabin of a ship, stranded in the bitter, harsh and
bleak ice of the north never quite goes away with these other settings across Europe.

Point of view

There are three narratives, each new one embedded within the previous one. So the
story is told in the first person, with the exception of Felix's story (told in the third
person), which the creature relates to Victor Frankenstein. Despite these embedded
narratives and the potential for reported speech, the first person remains constant and
uncomplicated. If students find this confusing, they should consider reflecting on the
activities in this guide designed to have students think about narration and point of
view in literature.

Character development

Victor is initially filled with life, optimism, and fascination. This gradually turns into
obsession, however, and this leads to feelings of guilt, remorse and, ultimately, fear
and revenge. Whereas in the beginning he was directing his passions towards nature
and his intellect at scientific analysis, he later completely loses his capacity for
voluntary thought.

At the moment of his creation, the creature likely an innocent being. He is
subsequently altered by the continual rejections he suffers. He develops knowledge
as a result of learning language, discovering books and observing the family at the
cottage, and he becomes very clear about his condition, capable of great reflection.
He he alternates between compulsive, childlike behavior (but with the strength of a
man), compassionate understanding and vicious rage. Ultimately, his sadness at the
end of the novel reflects a complex individual.

Walton's lust for discovery makes him an early parallel to Victor's character, but his
ultimate decision to take his ship south marks a positive development in his
character, and makes him a foil to Victor Frankenstein.

Themes

Storytelling

Whether they are writing letters or reporting the events of their lives to others in person, the characters in the novel are narrators; they play the roles of raconteurs. The text is also filled with allusions to other works, some of which reflect the events of the text, enhancing the power of stories to shape our lives. The novel itself was a product of the author's participation in a weekend of storytelling.

Promethean Hubris

The story was originally called *Frankenstein; or The Modern Prometheus,* capturing the novel's obvious reflection of the Titan, Prometheus, who created humankind. Prometheus was punished (eternally) for stealing fire from the gods and giving it to humanity. Victor Frankenstein suffers a similar fate as the result of his creation.

The Laws of Nature

Intertwined with the Promethean theme is the point where human ingenuity clashes with the laws of nature. While Victor Frankenstein has found a way to control nature, he is himself situated within it, and he is himself subject to the consequences of these laws. This raises the questions of morality which Frankenstein becomes painfully aware of but which he ignores, possessed by his thirst to achieve all that is scientifically possible. Walton suffers from a mild form of this madness which Frankenstein exemplifies and which the creature embodies. They all confront and are to differing degrees seduced by the power of nature over them.

Responsibility and Free Will

What is Victor's responsibility to the creature? He rejects the creature immediately, but he is just as soon tormented by his confused sense of responsibility for the creature, and for what the creature does. This is particularly intense after William's death and during the trial of Justine. Is the creature responsible for the deaths, or is he responsible for them? Did the creature have free will or can he blame his creator? Additionally, did Victor know what he was doing when he made the creature, or was he possessed by the forces of his creator? How responsible are the characters in the story for the way their actions impact others? This is the question that surely faced Walton before he decided to turn his ship around.

Symbols

Electricity

For Victor, the laws of electricity are the keys to knowledge of and control of the elements. For Victor, that knowledge life, but it is also destruction. Lightening helps to represent this symbolism in the story.

Fire

Fire is a symbol of survival. The creature discovers fire, and with it he has extended his life.

The Creature's Eye

The eyes are the windows to the soul. When the creature's eye opens, Victor realizes he has done more than create life biologically speaking. He has created something much greater. He has created consciousness.

Climax

There are several events in volume three which feel like structural turning points, including when he destroys his second creation and when Elizabeth is murdered. These two can be interpreted as the climax for different reasons. Killing the second creation is arguably the turning point in the story. Victor cannot go back, and it seems as though he has sealed his fate. Elizabeth's death marks the falling action of the story, which at that point becomes a chase that is never fulfilled.

Structure

The plot structure is driven by the changes in narration. The longest narrative (Victor's) is told in retrospect. And he begins with his family's origins. He presents the situations of his childhood and education leading up to the conflict that sets dramatic events in motion. His moment of conscience (the moment he realizes he has created a monster he wants nothing to do with) marks the conflict's beginning and is the start of the story's ongoing tension. The creature's development further complicates the plot, as we begin to question who the victim is (Victor or the creature, or Victor's family, or everyone). The unresolved tension between the creature and his creator becomes more intense with the decision to destroy the second experiment. Here, the suspense shifts from fulfilling the wishes of the creature to protecting everyone from the creature's wrath. The chase begins after Elizabeth's death, and the story's conclusion is marked by the death of the main narrator (Victor), the vanishing of the creature and the resolution of Walton (the one who set the stage for the story) to go home.

Teacher Guide - Relationship to Other Books

Consider using the texts referred to or alluded to within the novel:

- The Myth of Prometheus
- Milton's *Paradise Lost*
- Coleridge's "Rime of the Ancient Mariner"
- Plutarch's *Lives*
- Goethe's *The Sorrows of Young Werther*
- Constantin-Francois Volney's *Ruins of Empires*

Consider the following complimentary novels:

- Bram Stoker's *Dracula*
- Robert Louis Stevenson's *The Strange Case of Dr. Jekyll and Mr. Hyde*
- Mary Shelley's *The Last Man*

In addition to the following texts below about *Frankenstein*, see "Further Reading" at the back of the text that is used for this guide.

- William St Clair's *The Godwins and the Shelleys: The Biography of a Family*
- Harold Bloom's *Frankenstein, or the New Prometheus', Partisan Review 32*
- Pamela Clemit's *The Godwinian Novel: The Rational Fictions of Godwin, Brockden Brown, Mary Shelley*

Teacher Guide - Bringing in Technology

In multiple activities in this guide (starting with the travelogue activity in Day 1), students should consider using Voicethread, Evernote, Google Docs or other digital tools to carry out interactive writing journals.

Consider using video (which you can access in the tools above) to capture the Interview with the Creature activity in Day 3.

Use Google Gallery for the Visual Art activity in Day 5.

Consider using popular story-boarding software for the activity in Day 2.

Use the internet for research on multiple HW assignments, and especially on for the Cultural History research in Day 1.

Teacher Guide - Notes to the Teacher

The text selected for this guide uses three volumes. Each volume begins with a first chapter. Whether it is vocabulary or the reading assignment instructions, be sure to notice what volume the chapter corresponds to. This is noted in the reading assignment tab for each of the five Days in the guide.

The lessons and activities in this guide provide a variety of approaches to the themes of *Frankenstein;* select those that best suit the strengths and interests of your own class.

The short answer questions in this guide are meant to test reading recall and mainly cover concrete facts in the reading. The thought questions are meant to stimulate discussion. Some are interpretive and others ask students to recall concrete information from the story. Customize them at your will, or re-purpose them as essay questions for the end of the unit. If you choose to re-purpose them in this way, students should develop more formal responses than the ones they may come up with in class.

The questions provided for the final essays and the final paper may be used as they are written in this guide, or they may be adapted in a way that encourages students to write on topics that have been discussed in class. The papers should be written in the more formal writing style expected in a literary essay. At the same time, students should not be discouraged from choosing their own topics. Remember that grading an essay should not depend on a simple checklist of required content, but should take a holistic approach to understanding. Use the rubric provided.

Teacher Guide - Related Links

The Literature Network

http://www.online-literature.com/shelley_mary/

Background and information about Mary Shelley.

Romantic Circles

http://www.rc.umd.edu/editions/mws/immortal/index.html

A refereed scholarly Website devoted to the study of Romantic-period literature and culture.

Frankensteinia

http://frankensteinia.blogspot.com/

A blog of references and popular culture allusions to the *Frankenstein* legacy.

Teacher Guide - Frankenstein Bibliography

Lucas Duclos, author of Lesson Plan. Completed on April 21, 2016, copyright held by GradeSaver.

Updated and revised by Ellie Campisano April 30, 2016. Copyright held by GradeSaver.

Mary Shelley. Frankenstein, or The Modern Prometheus (Edited with an Introduction and Notes by Maurice Hindle). London: Penguin Classics, 2003.

John Milton. The Poetical Works of John Milton. http://www.gutenberg.org: Project Gutenberg Press, 2009.

Samuel Taylor Coleridge. The Rime of the Ancient Mariner. www.gutenberg.org: Project Gutenberg Press, 2006.

https://www.gutenberg.org/files/84/84-h/84-h.htm

Neil Fraistat, Elizabeth Denlinger, and Raffaele Viglianti. "The Shelley-Godwin Archive." The British Library . Curated continually.. March 2016. <http://shelleygodwinarchive.org/>.

Day 1 - Reading Assignment, Questions, Vocabulary

Read from **Letter 1** through **Chapter 3** of Volume 1.

Common Core Objectives

- CCSS.ELA-Literacy.CCRA.R.2 Determine central ideas or themes of a text and analyze their development; summarize the key supporting details and ideas.

- CCSS.ELA-Literacy.CCRA.W.3 Write narratives to develop real or imagined experiences or events using effective technique, well-chosen details and well-structured event sequences.

Note that it is perfectly fine to expand any day's work into two days depending on the characteristics of the class, particularly if the class will engage in all of the suggested classroom exercises and activities and discuss all of the thought questions.

Content Summary for Teachers

Letter 1 - Chapter 3 (Volume 1)

The Letters

The story begins with Walton's four letters to his sister, Margaret. Walton shares some of the details of the beginning of his journey to the North Pole, a destination that symbolizes his yearning to achieve something great in his life. Walton discusses his longing for companionship —for someone with whom he can share his passion for adventure. Walton reports witnessing a strange occurrence after the ship stalls amidst the ice flows. They observe a large figure being pulled by a sled in the distance. A day later, they see another sled, only this time the man is not as large, and many of his dogs are dead. This is Victor Frankenstein, and Walton takes him in. After a couple of days of convalescence, Frankenstein agrees to tell Walton his story.

Chapter 1

Frankenstein commences his narrative. He explains how his father came to meet and become married to Caroline, the daughter of his late friend, Beaufort. The two of them traveled regularly, finally giving birth to Victor in Italy. Caroline adopts a Elizabeth, who is living with a very poor family. She becomes Victor's beloved sister.

Chapter 2

Frankenstein relates his happy childhood relationships with Elizabeth and his friend, Henry Clerval back in Switzerland, where his parents gave birth to another son. Later, he becomes passionate about the natural world. An avid student of natural philosophy and literature of the alchemists, he becomes curious about the nature of life and death.

Chapter 3

At seventeen, Victor is prepared to attend university at Ingolstadt. Before he leaves, Elizabeth becomes sick. Caroline tends to her, and she finally recovers, but as a result of her close contact, Caroline becomes sick and dies. Before passing away, she expresses to Victor and Elizabeth her hopes that they will marry. Before Victor leaves for school, Clerval visits him and expresses his wishes that he could go as well. He explains that his father has other more practical plans for him. Victor is sad to leave and for a short time he becomes nostalgic about his life at home with Elizabeth and Clerval. But along his journey, he becomes filled with desire for more knowledge. At Ingolstadt, Victor meets Krempe, a professor of natural philosophy who tells Victor that he must begin to study the sciences, and this is a suggestion reinforced by Victor's fascination with professor Waldman.

Thought Questions (students consider while they read)

1. What are some of the things Robert Walton longs for, and how does the character of Frankenstein answer and respond to these longing?

2. What is the significance of the story structure that is set up in these letters and early chapters?

3. What is Victor Frankenstein as narrator expressing about human relationships in the opening of his own narrative, and what might this be foreshadowing?

4. What are some signs of Victor's potentially destructive interest or obsession with science, and what are some aspects of Victor's early life which helped to tame that obsession?

5. How does Victor's journey away from home to Ingolstadt mark a difficult but positive growth for him?

Vocabulary (in order of appearance)

"You will rejoice to hear that no disaster has accompanied the commencement of an enterprise which you have regarded with such evil forebodings," Letter One

forebodings:

fears of bad things to come

"Inspirited by this wind of promise, my day dreams become more fervent and vivid," Letter One

fervant:

intensely passionate

"I am about to proceed on a long and difficult voyage, the emergencies of which will demand all my fortitude," Letter One

fortitude:

strength

"I have no one near me, gentle yet courageous, possessed of a cultivated as well as of a capacious mind," Letter Two

capacious:

having a lot of room inside

open-minded

"Yet some feelings, unallied to the dross of human nature, beat even in these rugged bosoms," Letter Two

dross:

garbage or rubbish

"He was respected by all who knew him, for his integrity and indefatigable attention to public business," Chapter One

indefatigable:

enduring tirelessly

"I desire, therefore, in this narration, to state those facts which led to my predilection for that science," Chapter Two

predilection:

a preference for or inclination towards

"...and that a modern system of science had been introduced, which possessed much greater powers than the ancient, because the powers of the latter were chimerical, while those of the former were real and practical," Chapter Two

chimerical:

imaginary or unreal

"...who, when he found the father inexorable, quitted his country, nor returned until he heard that his former mistress was married according to her inclinations," Chapter Two

inexorable:

impossible to prevent

"I will be cool, persevering and prudent," Chapter Three

prudent:

acting with care for the consequences

Additional Homework

1. Ask students to do casual research online, looking for information about the period during which the text was written (early nineteenth century). Have them identify qualities of R. Walton which seem to reflect the general spirit and mood of that time.

Day 1 - Discussion of Thought Questions

1. What are some of the things Robert Walton longs for, and how does the character of Frankenstein answer and respond to these longing?

Time:

10-15 min

Discussion:

Students should discuss Walton's longing for companionship along his journey, and they should observe how the insertion of Frankenstein as a character begins to satisfy that desire. They should also discuss Walton's desire for exploration and discovery, despite potential risks and costs. They should then observe what Frankenstein has to say about lust for knowledge and adventure.

2. What is the significance of the story structure that is set up in these letters and early chapters?

Time:

10-15 min

Discussion:

Students should describe the layered structure of the narrative, observing the relationship between the narrators and their audience. These should include Walton as narrator and Margaret as audience, and then Frankenstein/Walton, etc. Strong answers will interpret the effect this shifting focus has on the reader. Possible interpretations might consider the parallels between the narratives, looking at themes that each of them share. These might include companionship and the thirst for knowledge and domination. They may also consider the background of the novel as a ghost story — the frame narrative making the reader aware of their own participation as audience.

3. What is Victor Frankenstein as narrator expressing about human relationships in the opening of his own narrative, and what might this be foreshadowing?

Time:

5-10 min

Discussion:

Strong answers should observe the focus on family, and then go on to discuss narrative's emphasis on the responsibilities of loved ones to each other. They should discuss the way the family comes together, noticing the parallels between the elder Frankenstein taking in Caroline, and the family later taking in Elizabeth. They should observe the way those who are in need are adopted into the family. They should make informed predictions about where this could go for Victor.

4. What are some signs of Victor's potentially destructive interest or obsession with science, and what are some aspects of Victor's early life which helped to tame that obsession?

Time:

10-15 min

Discussion:

Strong answers will look at his fascination with natural events and the texts of the alchemists, noticing his tendeny to become consumed by ideas and retreat from human contact in the process. Students should discuss his family values which were set up by the narrative in Chapter 1. They may interpret his relationship with Elizabeth as one that grounds him in everyday delights. This discussion should also include his relationship with Henry Clerval, an intellectual a little less prone to impassioned whims and fancies. Students should also discuss nature's effects on Victor, observing that while it inspires his creativity, it also provides a sense of well-being.

5. How does Victor's journey away from home to Ingolstadt mark a difficult but positive growth for him?

Time:

5-10 min

Discussion:

Students should discuss the significance of Victor's relationship with Henry and Elizabeth. They should observe his mother's death and the strong connection created with Elizabeth afterwards. They may interpret this as an inner journey away from a stable side of his life which grounded him, but which he sees as something that also held him back intellectually. They should then observe that because he knows no one at Ingolstadt, which at first concerns him, he will therefore devote himself to his works completely.

Day 1 - Short Answer Evaluation

1. Who are these letters addressed to?

   Margaret, sister of Robert Walton

2. What does Walton say that he lacks and wish he had on his trip?

   A friend, someone to share things with

3. What strange thing did he report seeing?

   A large figure, in a sledge, guiding dogs

4. What did the stranger ask Walton before he agreed to come aboard?

   Asked where they were going

5. Where was Victor Frankenstein born?

   Geneva, Switzerland

6. What science (branch of study) did Frankenstein have a predelection for?

   Natural Philosophy

7. Where did Frankenstein go to university?

   Ingolstadt

8. What was Frankenstein's good friend at home?

   Henry Clerval

9. What did professor Krempe say was nonsense?

Work of alchemists

10. Who was much more appreciative of the authors Frankenstein had studied?

Professor Waldman

Answer Key

1. Margaret, the sister of Robert Walton.
2. A friend. Someone to share things with.
3. A large figure in a sledge, guiding dogs.
4. He asked them where they were going.
5. Geneva, Switzerland.
6. Natural Philosophy.
7. Ingolstadt.
8. Henry Clerval.
9. The work of the alchemists.
10. Professor Waldman.

Day 1 - Crossword Puzzle

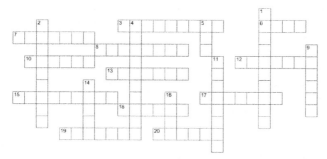

ACROSS

3. This girl enjoyed "wondrous scenes which surrounded our Swiss home"
6. The name of the mountains around Frankenstein's home
7. Frankenstein's close friend
8. Walton's sister
10. Frankenstein was born in this city
12. Walton referenced The Rime of the Ancient _____
13. _____ philosophy was the passion which regulated Frankenstein's fate
15. A branch of science Frankenstein found fascinating
17. In the north, the sun is "forever visible" and barely scrapes the _____
18. The stranger's first name
19. A large mass of floating ice
20. Isaac _____, a scientist with whom he shared a similar passion

DOWN

1. A place where a scientist performs experiments
2. At this age, it was determined Frankenstein would go to Ingolstadt
4. During a terrible storm at Belrive, they witnessed this electric phenomenon
5. The stranger did not speak for this many days
9. Walton was in need of a companion, or this
11. This woman became sick and died before Frankenstein left for school
14. They placed the stranger near this warm apparatus for cooking
16. Walton is headed to the North _____

Crossword Puzzle Answer Key

```
                                    ¹L
        ²S              ³E ⁴L I Z A B E ⁵T H    ⁶A L P S
⁷C L E R V A L             I              W     B
        V         ⁸M A R G A R E T        O     O        ⁹F
    ¹⁰G E N E V A          H              ¹¹C  ¹²M A R I N E R
        N         ¹³N A T U R A L          A     A        I
        T         ¹⁴S       E              R     T        E
¹⁵C H E M I S T R Y        ¹⁶N        ¹⁷H O R I Z O N     N
        E         O        ¹⁸V I C T O R   L     R        D
        N         V        L              I     Y
            ¹⁹I C E B E R G ²⁰N E W T O N  N
                           E
```

ACROSS

3. This girl enjoyed "wondrous scenes which surrounded our Swiss home"
6. The name of the mountains around Frankenstein's home
7. Frankenstein's close friend
8. Walton's sister
10. Frankenstein was born in this city
12. Walton referenced The Rime of the Ancient _____
13. _____ philosophy was the passion which regulated Frankenstein's fate
15. A branch of science Frankenstein found fascinating
17. In the north, the sun is "forever visible" and barely scrapes the _____
18. The stranger's first name
19. A large mass of floating ice
20. Isaac _____, a scientist with whom he shared a similar passion

DOWN

1. A place where a scientist performs experiments
2. At this age, it was determined Frankenstein would go to Ingolstadt
4. During a terrible storm at Belrive, they witnessed this electric phenomenon
5. The stranger did not speak for this many days
9. Walton was in need of a companion, or this
11. This woman became sick and died before Frankenstein left for school
14. They placed the stranger near this warm apparatus for cooking
16. Walton is headed to the North _____

Day 1 - Vocabulary Quiz

Terms

1. ___E___ forebodings
2. ___H___ fervant
3. ___C___ fortitude
4. ___G___ capacious
5. ___I___ dross
6. ___J___ indefatigable
7. ___D___ predilection
8. ___A___ chimerical
9. ___F___ inexorable
10. ___B___ prudent

Answers

A. imaginary or unreal
B. acting with care for the consequences
C. strength
D. a preference for or inclination towards
E. fears of bad things to come
F. impossible to prevent
G. roomy
H. intensely passionate
I. garbage or rubbish
J. enduring tirelessly

Answer Key

1. E forebodings: fears of bad things to come
2. H fervant: intensely passionate
3. C fortitude: strength
4. G capacious: roomy
5. I dross: garbage or rubbish
6. J indefatigable: enduring tirelessly
7. D predilection: a preference for or inclination towards
8. A chimerical: imaginary or unreal
9. F inexorable: impossible to prevent
10. B prudent: acting with care for the consequences

Day 1 - Classroom Activities

1. Travelogue

Kind of Activity:

Individual Writing

Objective:

Students will be able to record and recall significant details about setting, action and character.

Common Core Standards:

CCSS.ELA-Literacy.CCRA.R.3, CCSS.ELA-Literacy.CCRA.W.3

Time:

10-15 minutes (recurring)

Structure:

Have students begin a travelogue, recording things that happen in places along the story. As travelogues share not just details about places, but about experiences and impressions as well, students will record and interpret characters' inner thoughts.

With every changing setting, have students provide a description of

- Place
- Events
- Character Impressions (not included in the text)

Finally, have students include a final reflection on what they wrote.

Note: Students may do this in first person as the characters, or in third person as themselves commenting on this information as if they were there too.

Ideas for Differentiated Instruction:

For students who require more engaging, hands-on learning for such extended activities, consider doing this as a podcast and with student pairs, having them record the information conversationally. Use Voicethread, Evernote or some other audio technology that allows playback.

Assessment Ideas:

Students should post example passages from their travelogue on a course website or on a bulletin board. They may also want to read them aloud, or play them back (in the case that they were recorded podcasts/conversations).

2. Reading With Questions in Mind: Cultural History

Kind of Activity:

Group Work

Objective:

Students will be able to discuss the themes and events of the story in relation to the story's social and political climate.

Common Core Standards:

CCSS.ELA-Literacy.CCRA.R.2, CCSS.ELA-Literacy.CCRA.R.9

Time:

10-15 minutes (recurring)

Structure:

Consider doing this in pairs or groups.

Students should begin by defining the topic of their journal. Students may select a specific category (Science, Art, Politics, Philosophy), or one of the broader eras overlapping with or encapsulating the novel's publication/reception (Romanticism, Enlightenment). They may then journal across some of the more specific topics within that era. Students should write a brief synopsis on their topic, including references to important works, achievements, themes, events, etc.

Have students include 3-5 "Essential Questions" that address what they will be searching for as they read.

As they come across related themes in the text, have them write a brief but poignant reflection that responds to their questions, including relevant images or audio attachments (if using Evernote, Voicethread or Google Docs for the journal).

Ideas for Differentiated Instruction:

For students struggling to use technology for extended reading assignments, consider using a binder in which students can scrapbook connections they make between their research on their topic (Science for example) and the text.

For students who struggle with independent research, provide a list of possible topics, and ask them to do a report summarizing the topic. Have them highlight the text as they discover issues related to their report. Below are more specific suggestions:

- Science (Luigi Galvani, Giovanni Aldini, Humphry Davy and William Nicholson, Darwin, Ben Franklin)
- Philosophy (Locke, Rousseau, William Godwin, and Mary Wollstonecraft)
- Natural Philosophy
- European Imperialism
- Industrial revolution

Assessment Ideas:

Have students present their strongest textual references to the class. Do this for every chapter, after each unit, or after each of the five sections (Days) in this guide.

Day 2 - Reading Assignment, Questions, Vocabulary

Read **Chapter 4** through **Chapter 8** in Volume 1.

Common Core Objectives

- CCSS.ELA-Literacy.CCRA.W.3 Write narratives to develop real or imagined experiences or events using effective technique, well-chosen details and well-structured event sequences.

- CCSS.ELA-Literacy.CCRA.R.2 Determine central ideas or themes of a text and analyze their development; summarize the key supporting details and ideas.

Note that it is perfectly fine to expand any day's work into two days depending on the characteristics of the class, particularly if the class will engage in all of the suggested classroom exercises and activities and discuss all of the thought questions.

Content Summary for Teachers

Chapter 4 - 8 (Volume 1)

Chapter 4

Victor becomes immersed in his experiments, and he becomes particularly focused on chemistry. He works very closely with professor Waldman. He explores the nature of life, and this leads him to question and investigate how to animate the non-living. He discovers the secret of how to generate life through a sudden epiphany. He does not, however, share the content of this revelation with Walton (and, by extension, with the reader), because his own knowledge resulted in misery and destruction. He begins to assume the power of one who can bestow life on the dead. He collects body parts from cemeteries, and begins to construct his human being. In his narrative to Walton about this period, he expresses his awareness of his obsessive and destructive drive.

Chapter 5

Victor observes the creature coming to life. He is repulsed by his creation. He suddenly becomes aware of the nightmare that he has created. He retreats to his bedchamber. After the creature find him there, Victor abandons him and paces in the streets where he eventually runs into Clerval, who bears news that his family is worried about him. Victor returns to find that the creature is gone. He falls ill, and Henry becomes his caretaker.

Chapter 6

As Victor convalesces in a new apartment, removed from his scientific instruments, he studies poetry and literature with Henry, and reads letter from home. Seasons change, and Victor's travels in the countryside better his spirits and reignite a healthier relationship with the natural world.

Chapter 7

Victor receives a letter recounting the events surrounding William's death. Henry arranges for them to return to Geneva. On their way there, Victor is gripped by fear regarding William's murderer, and after glimpsing the creature in the light of a thunderstorm, his worry that it was the creature who murdered William is realized. Justine, the family servant who went searching for William after news he had disappeared, is accused of murdering him. Victor cannot bring himself to tell anyone about the creature's involvement, for fear they will find him (and the very idea of the creature) insane.

Chapter 8

As the trial gets underway, Victor his tortured by his guilty thoughts about the two innocent people that will have lost their lives because of his creation. The prosecutor makes a convincing case against Justine. On the stand, Justine explains how she had become wrapped up in the events surrounding William's death. Elizabeth takes the stand and advocates for Justine, though failing to sway the overwhelming opinion that she is guilty. Justine confesses to the crime to gain absolution. She is sentenced to death. Victor reflects on his responsibility for these tragedies.

Thought Questions (students consider while they read)

1. How does the effect of Victor's isolation from family and friends at Ingolstadt echo his warning to Walton earlier on?

2. Why is it both surprising and obvious that Victor rejects the creature he has created?

3. Do you find it unrealistic or unlikely (even despite the fantastical nature of the story) that the creature would just disappear? What is the rationale (of the author and of the story) for this fact?

4. What happens to Victor's health as a result of the events preceding and following the creatures birth, and what is the symbolism of Victor's worsening and improving health?

5. Why was Victor so sure that the creature was the murderer?

Vocabulary (in order of appearance)

"His gentleness was never tinged by dogmatism, and his instructions were given with an air of frankness and good nature, that banished every idea of pedantry." Chapter Four

pedantry:

overly concerned about rules

"In a thousand ways he smoothed for me the path of knowledge, and made the most abstruse enquiries clear and facile to my apprehension." Chapter Four

abstruse:

difficult to understand

"It surprised me, that what before was dese"In a thousand ways he smoothed for me the path of knowledge, and made the most abstruse enquiries clear and facile to my apprehension." Chapter Four

facile:

easily or superficially understood

"At length lassitude succeeded to the tumult I had before endured;" Chapter Five

lassitude:

physical or mental fatigue

"at others, I nearly sank to the ground through languor and extreme weakness." Chapter Five

languor:

a state of fatigue

"as children are accustomed to do when they expect a spectre to stand in waiting for them on the other side;" Chapter Five

spectre:

a ghost

"but the pertinacity with which I continually recurred to the same subject, persuaded him that my disorder indeed owed its origin to some uncommon and terrible event." Chapter Five

pertinacity:

stubbornly holding to an opinion

"He looks upon study as an odious fetter;" Chapter Six

odious:

very unpleasant

"Is this to prognosticate peace, or to mock at my unhappiness?" Chapter Seven

prognosticate:

to foretell

"but fear and hatred of the crime of which they supposed her guilty rendered them timorous, and unwilling to come forward." Chapter Eight

timorous:

fear and lack of confidence

Additional Homework

1. Have students write ten Google searches that Victor did throughout his experiments. Ask them to think creatively. Have them take notes on one of these results, and ask them to explain in class how Victor (or how his experiments) improved as a result of the search.

Day 2 - Discussion of Thought Questions

1. How does the effect of Victor's isolation from family and friends at Ingolstadt echo his warning to Walton earlier on?

Time:

5-10 min

Discussion:

Consider this discussion a natural evolution of the one preceding it in Day 1. Students should discuss Victor's isolation from his family as a driver of his growing obsession with natural philosophy and chemistry. They should observe that being alone over-inflates his thirst for knowledge to unhealthy proportions. Students may interpret his obsession to create a life as guided by his interest in some kind of deeper companionship (in addition to a passion for science). They may tie this back into Walton's own isolation and lust for knowledge.

2. Why is it both surprising and obvious that Victor rejects the creature he has created?

Time:

10-15 min

Discussion:

Strong answers will consider the contradictions in his rejection of the creature. They will discuss the kindness and inclusiveness of his family life, which was discussed earlier in the story. They should observe his family's own record of adoption, and they should look at his close relationships with Elizabeth and Henry as evidence that he is capable of deep affection for others (or at least was). They should also consider the obvious fact that he knew exactly what he was doing. However, this discussion should also observe his obsession and lack of reflection on the ethics of the task. They might explain that he seemed divorced from reality, which apparently became aware of later when the creature opened its eye, and when he realized he created a free-thinking individual.

3. Do you find it unrealistic or unlikely (even despite the fantastical nature of the story) that the creature would just disappear? What is the rationale (of the author and of the story) for this fact?

Time:

10-15 min

Discussion:

Answers will be subjective, but either way, strong answers should support their interpretation with a solid critique of events. Students may argue that this allows other events in the plot to take shape, and that we should not overly question such a small aspect of a fictional story. They should discuss those plot developments. Some may argue, for example, that this adds an emotional element to the story, amplifying the sense of rejection and reflecting Victor's own denial of his work and abandonment of an innocent life.

4. What happens to Victor's health as a result of the events preceding and following the creatures birth, and what is the symbolism of Victor's worsening and improving health?

Time:

10-15 min

Discussion:

Strong answers should observe the madness that accompanies Victor's obsession with his project. They should observe his own declaration that he would find amusements and exercises to stave of illness when he was through with his project. They should observe his illness following the events despite what he said and then explain that over time, and with the help of the more level-headed intellectual interests of Clerval, his health returns. Strong answers may argue that his sickness symbolizes the painful relationship between life and death: that breathing life into something almost took his own life away from him. They may argue that the kind of light associated with ideas and with knowledge revealed itself intensely, like the bolt of destructive lightning he witnessed earlier. They should discuss Victor's return to a more balanced idea of knowledge as something that ventilates the mind and foments understanding, as is brought about by Clerval's books and his walks in the country.

5. Why was Victor so sure that the creature was the murderer?

Time:

10-15 min

Discussion:

Students may question whether Victor had enough (or any) evidence to suggest that the creature murdered his brother. They may observe the weak correlation of people and events altogether. Strong answers should observe Victor's obsessive fears regarding the whereabouts of the creature. They should observe the thoughts he shares when he sees the creature, as stated here: "No sooner did that idea cross my imagination, than I became convinced of its truth ... The mere presence of the idea was an irresistible proof of the fact." Students may argue that this reflects Victor's madness, guilt and overwhelming sense of wrongdoing, and that these emotions serve his intuition more than his intellect.

Day 2 - Short Answer Evaluation

1. What specific discipline occupied nearly all of Frankenstein's time?

   _____

2. About how tall did Frankenstein resolve to make his being?

   _____

3. Why did Frankenstein promise himself to exercise and have fun when he was through with his endeavor?

   _____

4. What part of the creature was the first thing to show the sign of life?

   _____

5. Who was Frankenstein's only nurse during the period in which he fell ill?

   _____

6. Who wrote a letter to Frankenstein, showing great concern for his illness and abcense?

   _____

7. Whose works did Frankenstein find pleasure in reading while he was getting better?

   _____

8. What unfortunate news did Victor's father report to him in a letter?

   _____

9. What object was judged to be the temptation of William's murder?

_____

10. Why did Justine finally confess to the murder?

_____

Answer Key

1. Chemistry.
2. Eight feet.
3. He was working without rest, and he planned to drive away any incipient disease.
4. The eye. It's eye opened.
5. Henry Clerval.
6. Elizabeth.
7. The work of the "Orientalists," shared with him by Clerval.
8. William had died. He was murdered.
9. A locket containing a picture of their mother, Caroline.
10. She did it to obtain absolution.

Day 2 - Crossword Puzzle

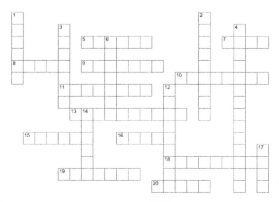

ACROSS

5. Another word for jail
7. In nature, his spirits were not low, but instead were _____
8. The creature was about this many feet in hight
9. Frankenstein's brother
10. He may have been referred to as a monster, or the _____
11. Frankenstein's brother was killed, or this
13. A branch of biology dealing with the functioning of living organisms
15. Elizabeth was both the cousin of the murdered child, and the _____ as well
16. Clerval called forth the better feelings not of Frankenstein's head but his _____
18. Frankenstein wanted to bestow this upon matter, or another word for movement
19. A surprising and unexplainable event thought to be the work of a divine agency
20. Unusually high body temperature, or this

DOWN

1. The months of this warm season passed while Frankenstein was at work
2. Frankenstein's unhealthy thirst or for this turned out to be dangerous
3. In this branch of science, you might have to dissect the body of an organism
4. None of the judges liked to condemn a criminal by this kind of evidence
6. Another word for sickness
12. Frankenstein's wonderful dream turned into this instead
14. Another word for terror
17. The Swiss mountains that never changed were clad in this

Crossword Puzzle Answer Key

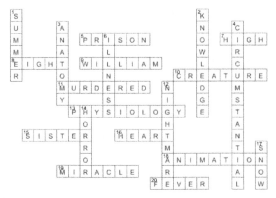

ACROSS

5. Another word for jail
7. In nature, his spirits were not low, but instead were _____
8. The creature was about this many feet in hight
9. Frankenstein's brother
10. He may have been referred to as a monster, or the _____
11. Frankenstein's brother was killed, or this
13. A branch of biology dealing with the functioning of living organisms
15. Elizabeth was both the cousin of the murdered child, and the _____ as well
16. Clerval called forth the better feelings not of Frankenstein's head but his _____
18. Frankenstein wanted to bestow this upon matter, or another word for movement
19. A surprising and unexplainable event thought to be the work of a divine agency
20. Unusually high body temperature, or this

DOWN

1. The months of this warm season passed while Frankenstein was at work
2. Frankenstein's unhealthy thirst or for this turned out to be dangerous
3. In this branch of science, you might have to dissect the body of an organism
4. None of the judges liked to condemn a criminal by this kind of evidence
6. Another word for sickness
12. Frankenstein's wonderful dream turned into this instead
14. Another word for terror
17. The Swiss mountains that never changed were clad in this

Day 2 - Vocabulary Quiz

Terms

1. _____ pedantry
2. _____ abstruse
3. _____ facile
4. _____ lassitude
5. _____ languor
6. _____ spectre
7. _____ pertinacity
8. _____ odious
9. _____ prognosticate
10. _____ timorous

Answers

A. difficult to understand
B. overly concerned about rules
C. stubbornly holding to an opinion
D. a ghost
E. a state of fatigue
F. to foretell
G. very unpleasant
H. physical or mental fatigue
I. fear and lack of confidence
J. easily or superficially understood

Answer Key

1. B pedantry: overly concerned about rules
2. A abstruse: difficult to understand
3. J facile: easily or superficially understood
4. H lassitude: physical or mental fatigue
5. E languor: a state of fatigue
6. D spectre: a ghost
7. C pertinacity: stubbornly holding to an opinion
8. G odious: very unpleasant
9. F prognosticate: to foretell
10. I timorous: fear and lack of confidence

Day 2 - Classroom Activities

1. Storyboards

Kind of Activity:

Mixed Media

Objective:

Stuents will be able to analyize the plot.

Common Core Standards:

CCSS.ELA-Literacy.CCRA.R.3, CCSS.ELA-Literacy.CCRA.W.3

Time:

30-35 minutes

Structure:

Storyboards are a good way to visualize stories, capture and analyze significant text (both narration and dialogue). They can also be a good way to discuss changes in setting and in dramatic sequences of events. As this section of the reading is filled with all of this, have students storyboard each chapter (4 through 8).

They are often used to brainstorm a the scenes of a motion picture. Consider following this activity with the Tableau Activity in this section (having students do dramatic tableau of scenes they storyboard).

Have students create graphic organizers to display their sequenced events from one of the chapter in this section. Here is a link to help learn more about story-boarding.

Include the following elements for each box in the storyboard:

1. A rough sketch inside the box.
2. Quotes inside the box or above the box.
3. Narration below the box.

Students should use as many pages or boxes as the need to, depending on the complexity of the scene or the amount of time they have for the activity.

Consider consulting the following list of storyboard generators online.

Have students interpret the cause/effect relationship between boxes.

Ideas for Differentiated Instruction:

For students who struggle with organizing ideas graphically, provide the option to pair up, and to have one student design the plates and the other select important text. Also consider having these students search for photographs or images online that may compliment the scenes used in the storyboard. They can add these images to the storyboard or put them on the back of the cards they will make for the assessment below.

Assessment Ideas:

Have students cut around their boxes so that they are now like cards. Have them mix up the cards and ask others to put them in order.

2. Dramatic Tableau

Kind of Activity:

Group Work

Objective:

Students will be able to discuss character's thoughts and motivations.

Common Core Standards:

CCSS.ELA-Literacy.CCRA.R.2

Time:

30-35 minutes

Structure:

Introduce students to the concept of tableau. Consider the following resource, here.

Ask students to choose a sequences of events from the storyboard activity in this section. These may be powerful action sequences or they may be powerful images, rich with opportunities for interpretation.

In groups, ask students to explore how to act out a scene. Then ask them to freeze at pivotal moments. This will be the freeze-frame that they and other students analyze and discuss. Students will play the role of characters, but they may also act as inanimate objects.

Practice quietly for about 15 minutes, and then perform the tableau for the class.

Have students take photographs of each other during the activity as they are performing. Use the photographs for the assessment below.

Onlooking students should be guided through the following questions:

1. What is happening in the scene overall.
2. What is each participant going through, thinking, doing? What are they doing and why are they doing it?
3. What happens if one of those things is taken out or changes? In this case, onlooking students can ask the the tableau actors to make a change, and then stay still so the class can reassess the scene.

Then, ask onlooking students to tap any characters in the tableau whose place they want to play in a different way. Then go over the questions above again. This is a way to extend the activity and discuss alternative ways the story could unfold.

Ideas for Differentiated Instruction:

For students who struggle to engage in this kind of interactive activity, provide the option to draw a still from the scene, or to use one of the photographs of the scene, and then have them apply the three steps in this activity to the scene they've drawn.

Assessment Ideas:

Have students assess, analyze, and write captions for the photographs taken of each group's tableau. Ask them to discuss ideas, insights and questions that came up which did not come up during the storyboard activity.

Day 3 - Reading Assignment, Questions, Vocabulary

Read **Chapter 1** through **Chapter 5** in Volume 2. (This would correspond to **Chapters 9** though **13** in texts that do not have the three volumes.)

Common Core Objectives

- CCSS.ELA-Literacy.CCRA.R.3 Analyze how and why individuals, events, or ideas develop and interact over the course of a text.

- CCSS.ELA-Literacy.CCRA.R.6 Assess how point of view or purpose shapes the content and style of a text.

Note that it is perfectly fine to expand any day's work into two days depending on the characteristics of the class, particularly if the class will engage in all of the suggested classroom exercises and activities and discuss all of the thought questions.

Content Summary for Teachers

Chapter 1 - 5 (Volume 2)

Chapter 1

Plagued with grief, the Frankensteins go to their house in Belrive. Contemplating suicide in the beautiful natural surroundings of Belrive, Victor becomes obsessed with his guilt, fear and revenge regarding the creature. Elizabeth's worldview is shattered by the tragedies, and she feels great pity for the man who must carry the guilt for William's murder on his conscience. Victor despairs when he hears her say this, as he feels that he is the man who must bear that guilt. Victor hikes through the mountains of Chamonix to relieve his suffering. The energy he exerts and the relief he feels in considering the omnipotent creator of such a majestic scene make it easier for him to rest and sleep.

Chapter 2

Victor determines to climb to the top of Montanvert, one of the region's massive glaciers. The grandeur of the mountains impresses on him feelings of joy and ecstasy, as he contemplates his place (and the place of all of humankind) in a world capable of creating such terrain. There, he encounters the creature, who says that he will continue his revenge against his creator if he does not consider his plight. The creature persuades Victor to listen to his story.

Chapter 3

The creature explains what it was like to be abandoned without understanding the world around him. He talks about his cold days and nights without food and shelter. With the same ecstatic astonishment that primitive man must have felt, the creature discovers fire. He shares the horror others express at the site of him. He comes across a cottage in the woods, and he crawls into a hovel there, where he can observe the family of three living inside — a young man, young woman, and older man. They become dear to him, and he explains how the qualities of language, music and love are revealed to him through a hole in the wall.

Chapter 4

The creature shares his desire to have reached out to the people of the cottage, who would surely treat him differently than the villagers who have rejected him. He hesitates so that he can learn more about them. He notices that they often seem sad, and he realizes they are living in poverty. He begins to do work for them, leaving the spoils of his efforts for them outside the house. He becomes more perceptive of the use of and meaning of words.

Chapter 5

In the Spring, a guest arrives at the cottage. It is the beautiful Safie, and she is there to see the young man, Felix. He notices that she speaks a different language, and the he develops his own language skills watching the family teach their language to her. They use a text called *Ruins of Empires*, and through this text the creature learns both language and history. His newfound knowledge about some of the darker aspects of human nature puts his own short and painful life into perspective concerning the atrocities humans are capable of, making him sure that the cottagers will never accept him. He feels great despair.

Thought Questions (students consider while they read)

1. How do characters change as a result of the tragedies in Volume 1?

2. Is Victor justified in his reaction to the creature when they run into each other?

3. What change occurs in the narration and what is the overall effect of this?

4. Why do you think Shelley decided to put the creature in the hovel, looking through the hole?

5. How does the creature's narrative contradict the idea Victor has of him?

Vocabulary (in order of appearance)

"I had an oscure feeling that all was not over, and that he would still commit some signal crime, which by its enormity should almost efface the recollection of the past," Chapter One

efface:

destroy or wipe out

"My abhorrence of this fiend cannot be conceived," Chapter One

abhorrence:

hatred

"Sometimes I could cope with the sullen despair that overwhelmed me," Chapter One

sullen:

depressive, sad

"I was benevolent and good; misery made me a fiend," Chapter Two

benevolent:

kind

"Before, dark and opaque bodies had surrounded me, impervious to my touch or sight," Chapter Three

impervious:

incapable of being penetrated

"the appearance was disconsolate, and I found my feet chilled by the cold damp outside that covered the ground," Chapter Three

disconsolate:

unhappy and without consolation

"Here then I retreated, and lay down happy to have found a shelter, however miserable, from the inclemency of the season," Chapter Three

inclemency:

bad weather

"...yet surely the gentle ass whose intentions were affectionate, although his manners were rude, deserved better treatment than blows and execration," Chapter Four

execration:

expression of great loathing for

"He appeared at one time a mere scion of the evil principle, and at another as all that can be conceived as noble and godlike," Chapter Five

scion:

a descendant

"It surprised me, that what before was desert and gloomy should now bloom with the most beautiful flowers and verdure," Chapter Five

verdure:

lush, green vegetation

Additional Homework

1. Have students read and bring in an article on one of the following topics:

    ◦ the human discovery and control of fire
    ◦ the development of language

   In class, have students discuss what it must have been like for the creature to develop these skills in light of the research they did.

Day 3 - Discussion of Thought Questions

1. How do characters change as a result of the tragedies in Volume 1?

Time:

10-15 min

Discussion:

Strong answers should consider all the characters who are most effected by the deaths of William and Justine, from the elder Frankenstein to Victor himself. But they should notice and discuss characters who undergo the deepest changes. These include Justine and Victor. They should discuss Justine's loss of innocence as result of tragedies that she had only read about or heard about before. They should consider the combination of guilt and conscience that develop in Victor, who has lost interest in or is completely averse to the impassioned research that once defined him. They should look for evidence of permanent change in Victor.

2. Is Victor justified in his reaction to the creature when they run into each other?

Time:

10-15 min

Discussion:

Answers will be subjective, but as usual, they should provide supporting evidence. Discussions should observe how Victor rejects and threatens the creature. They should discuss the details of the creature's response, including an analysis of the creature's request for Victor to simply hear his story. They may defend Victor's disparaging reaction in light of the horrible events, but they should also remember that Victor grasps his responsibility for these events. They may discuss how they are swayed by the creature's story, which further increases readers' sympathies for the creature.

3. What change occurs in the narration and what is the overall effect of this?

Time:

10-15 min

Discussion:

Discussions must notice the narration shift from Victor (who is telling his story to Walton) to the creature (who tells his story to Victor). They should observe this as a layering of one narrative within another. In other words, they should discuss the fact that it is still written in the first person, and they should explain the impact of the consistency of this point of view. They should consider how it develops sympathy for the creature. They may discuss how it would read if Victor reported the creature's story in the third person.

4. Why do you think Shelley decided to put the creature in the hovel, looking through the hole?

Time:

10-15 min

Discussion:

Strong answers will discuss how this part of the story serves to advance the plot in a very specific way. They should discuss how this helps the creature to learn human language and behavior. They should discuss the details of his education. They should observe that the creature, who is rejected by everyone else, needs a way to express himself at the same time, and could not have done so without either observing others or engaging in a complex relationship with them. They may argue that this aspect of the story strikes a balance between isolation (and abandonment) and socialization.

5. How does the creature's narrative contradict the idea Victor has of him?

Time:

10-15 min

Discussion:

Strong answers will analyze the language the creature uses. They will observe its sophistication, its richness of vocabulary and emotion, and the kind of deep intellect behind it. They should describe the narrative as one that contrasts with the earlier ideas of the creature as an unthinking monster. They should also consider the creature's message and appeal to conscience as a reflection of an intelligent and potentially logical being, contradicting Victor's idea of him as an irrational animal at best. They may, however, also argue that simply understanding his predicament does not excuse the monster from his heinous deeds.

Day 3 - Short Answer Evaluation

1. What terrible thing was Victor tempted to do when he was hiking in the mountains?

   _____

2. What wounded animal did Victor compare himself to?

   _____

3. What village did Victor finally arrive at, where he would sleep soundly again?

   _____

4. What did Victor say to the creature when they met?

   _____

5. What motivated Victor to listen to the creature's story?

   _____

6. What discovery did the creature find both alluring and useful to his survival?

   _____

7. What was something the cottagers did at night which the creature did not understand?

   _____

8. What evil did the creature realize was the cause of the cottager's distress?

   _____

9. Who was "the sweet Arabian?"

_____

10. Why didn't the creature attempt to meet the cottagers earlier on?

_____

Answer Key

1. Jump off a ledge. Commit suicide.
2. Deer.
3. Chamounix
4. He told him to go away, and that he would kill him to avenge William and Justine's death.
5. He wanted confirmation or denial of his opinion that the creature killed his brother; he also began to feel responsible for the creature's wickedness or happiness.
6. Fire.
7. They read aloud.
8. Poverty.
9. Safie. The visitor to the cottage.
10. He was afraid they would react as others had; he wanted to develop stronger language skills and learn more from them.

Day 3 - Crossword Puzzle

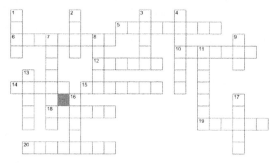

ACROSS

5. After a long time, Frankenstein arrived at this French-sounding village
6. Frankenstein heard the rumbling of this waterfall of snow
10. Another word for maker
12. Frankenstein spent some time roaming between the mountains, or this low area
14. A dark _____ brooded over him after Justine's death
15. There was a slowly advancing river of ice, or this massive landform
18. The old man took out this instrument and began to play
19. This season of thawing advanced rapidly
20. Another word for isolation

DOWN

1. The creature compared himself to this biblical first man
2. Exhaustion turned to extreme fatigue of body and _____
3. The beautiful Arabian
4. Frankenstein was tempted to commit this
7. The creature learned communication with words, or this
8. The creature lived in this small, squalid dwelling
9. Immersed in the mountains, Frankenstein's heart swelled with this wonderful feeling
11. The book from which Felix instructed Safie was The Ruins of _____
13. He did not get any shut-eye - aka _____ - for a while
16. The old man had lost this sense
17. Frankenstein felt responsible for his monster, and, therefore, this complex emotion

Crossword Puzzle Answer Key

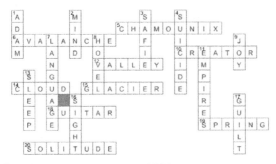

ACROSS

5. After a long time, Frankenstein arrived at this French-sounding village
6. Frankenstein heard the rumbling of this waterfall of snow
10. Another word for maker
12. Frankenstein spent some time roaming between the mountains, or this low area
14. A dark _____ brooded over him after Justine's death
15. There was a slowly advancing river of ice, or this massive landform
18. The old man took out this instrument and began to play
19. This season of thawing advanced rapidly
20. Another word for isolation

DOWN

1. The creature compared himself to this biblical first man
2. Exhaustion turned to extreme fatigue of body and _____
3. The beautiful Arabian
4. Frankenstein was tempted to commit this
7. The creature learned communication with words, or this
8. The creature lived in this small, squalid dwelling
9. Immersed in the mountains, Frankenstein's heart swelled with this wonderful feeling
11. The book from which Felix instructed Safie was The Ruins of _____
13. He did not get any shut-eye - aka _____ - for a while
16. The old man had lost this sense
17. Frankenstein felt responsible for his monster, and, therefore, this complex emotion

Day 3 - Vocabulary Quiz

Terms

1. _____ efface
2. _____ abhorrence
3. _____ sullen
4. _____ benevolent
5. _____ impervious
6. _____ disconsolate
7. _____ inclemency
8. _____ execration
9. _____ scion
10. _____ verdure

Answers

A. unhappy and without consolation
B. bad weather
C. hatred
D. kind
E. depressive, sad
F. expression of great loathing for
G. lush, green vegetation
H. destroy or wipe out
I. incapable of being penetrated
J. a descendant

Answer Key

1. H efface: destroy or wipe out
2. C abhorrence: hatred
3. E sullen: depressive, sad
4. D benevolent: kind
5. I impervious: incapable of being penetrated
6. A disconsolate: unhappy and without consolation
7. B inclemency: bad weather
8. F execration: expression of great loathing for
9. J scion: a descendant
10. G verdure: lush, green vegetation

Day 3 - Classroom Activities

1. Alternative Event

Kind of Activity:

Creative Writing

Objective:

Students will be able to discus the relationship between character development and plot.

Common Core Standards:

CCSS.ELA-Literacy.CCRA.R.3

Time:

50 min

Structure:

Students will play the role of Mary Shelley brainstorming ideas for her story. Specifically, they will write notes about how she came up with the idea to have the creature stay in a hovel, watching the family through a hole.

Have students begin by briefly summarizing the creature's life before the discovery of the cottage. Do not include the cottage in the summary.

Make sure students are familiar with the elements of plot structure, and especially the ways storytellers' develop their characters through conflic and tension in their plots. Also consider discussing the difference between story and plot (story being the events as they happened in real time, plot being the organization of those events in the text).

Students should then write a 1-2 pages of notes reflecting Shelley's thoughts about the following question: How can I get the creature to learn language and to learn about human culture?

in their notes, students should write about:

- the ways human beings learn language and culture
- what motivates the creature, where she would like the story to go, what aspects of the story depend on the creature's understanding of language and culture
- at least 2-3 ways the creature could have developed relationships with other people, discovered texts, etc.

Ideas for Differentiated Instruction:

For visual learners, or for learners who struggle to begin with an abstract goal, provide the option to create a Da Vinci style journal in which they sketch out things from Shelley's journal around the point when the creature discovers the cottage. They should also use the list above as a guide.

Assessment Ideas:

Have students present their (Shelley's) second best idea for this point in the plot. What else could have happened, given all the creature's problems, that would have helped him learn language and learn about human behavior?

2. Interview with The Creature

Kind of Activity:

Role Play

Objective:

Students will be able to demonstrate understanding of implicit and explicit meanings in the text.

Common Core Standards:

CCSS.ELA-Literacy.CCRA.R.6

Time:

50 min

Structure:

Have students conduct an interview with either the creature or with Victor. Students should ask three kinds of questions:

1. Questions to challenge the interviewee's comprehension of events in the text (looking for explicit meaning in the text)

   • Who took care of you while you were sick? (to Victor)

2. Questions that aim for answers you don't get directly from the text (implicit meaning)

   • Where did you go after you fled from the lab? (to the creature)
   • Why haven't you taken the creature's life? (to Victor)

3. Questions that require the interviewee to think creatively (subjective interpretation)

   • What do you have dreams about when you sleep? (to the creature)

Interviews should begin with a list of 10 questions. Answers should provide detailed description and evidence.

Ideas for Differentiated Instruction:

For students who struggle with multitasking alone, provide the option to record the interview with a partner. Students should simply set up a camera or audio device and record. Depending on how savvy they are with technology, they can include this in their travelogue journal.

Assessment Ideas:

Have students create a polished transcript of the interview. In the case that it was recorded, have them play the interview for the class.

Day 4 - Reading Assignment, Questions, Vocabulary

Read **Chapter 6** through **Chapter 9** in Volume 2. (This would correspond to **Chapters 14** through **17** in texts that do not use volumes.)

Common Core Objectives

- CCSS.ELA-Literacy.CCRA.R.3 Analyze how and why individuals, events, or ideas develop and interact over the course of a text.

- CCSS.ELA-Literacy.CCRA.SL.1 Prepare for and participate effectively in a range of conversations and collaborations with diverse partners, building on others' ideas and expressing their own clearly and persuasively.

- CCSS.ELA-Literacy.CCRA.R.1 Read closely to determine what the text says explicitly and to make logical inferences from it; cite specific textual evidence when writing or speaking to support conclusions drawn from the text.

Note that it is perfectly fine to expand any day's work into two days depending on the characteristics of the class, particularly if the class will engage in all of the suggested classroom exercises and activities and discuss all of the thought questions.

Content Summary for Teachers

Chapter 6 - 9 (Volume 2)

Chapter 6

The creature shares the cottager's personal history. The narration seems to take on another layer, focusing on the story that led the them to Germany and into poverty. Back in France, Felix promised a Turkish merchant that he would free him from his unjust imprisonment. In exchange, the merchant promised Felix his daughter's hand in marriage. Felix freed the merchant the night before his scheduled execution. As Felix was conducting the two fugitives across the French countryside, the French government threw Agatha and the elder De Lacey into prison. Felix returned to France, planning to return to the merchant's daughter, Safie, afterwards. They were stripped of their fortune and exiled. Despite the merchant's earlier plans to betray his promise to Felix, Safie and Felix were reunited in Germany.

Chapter 7

The creature is inspired by the family's commitment to one another. He also discovers Milton's *Paradise Lost*, Plutarch's *Lives*, and Goethe's *Sorrows of Werter*. He takes the both painful and uplifting events and themes of these texts to heart, and he compares himself to an abandoned Satan, rather than an Adam, watched over and loved. Soon after the discovery of the satchel, the creature finds Frankenstein's laboratory journal, and from this he becomes even more hopeless. But he resolves to approach the family, starting with the blind man. After a successful encounter with the him, the rest of the family arrives and casts the creature out of the house.

Chapter 8

Fleeing humankind (both literally and symbolically), the creature feels as though this last rejection is the final straw. He decides to exact revenge on his creator and on all of humankind. He returns to the cottage, hoping to win over the family through an another appeal to the older man, but learns that they are never coming back. He burns down the cottage. Having discovered the whereabouts of the Frankenstein before, he goes to Geneva to get revenge. After a long and arduous journey, the creature rescues a girl who falls into the water, only to be attacked by a man thereafter. The creature continues his story about how he killed William. He runs into William in Geneva. Fearful of the creature, William tells him that the elder Frankenstein will come after the creature. After failing to make William's acquaintance peacefully, and vengeful of his creator, he strangles the young boy who is apparently a relative of Victor's. He takes the locket, and he later places the locket in the possession of Justine, lying asleep in a barn. The creature explains why it is only fair to him that she should suffer the consequences of his horrible treatment, and he asks Frankenstein to make him an ugly companion who will not abandon him.

Chapter 9

Victor picks up the narration again. He expresses both understanding and disgust in regard to the creature's plight and request. Conflicted, he finally agrees to comply with what are more like demands than requests. The creature explains that he will stay abreast of Frankenstein's progress with the plan, and he goes away. Frankenstein returns to Geneva.

Thought Questions (students consider while they read)

1. What mixed signals does the creature get about humankind from the time he spends observing the cottagers?

2. What role does the creature's education play in his behavior and convictions?

3. Do you find the creature's responses to events fair or irrational and unjustified?

4. What is so tactful about the way the creature convinces Frankenstein to to help him?

5. What does the creature need in a companion, and do you think it would work out for him given the events so far?

Vocabulary (in order of appearance)

"She thanked him in the most ardent terms for his intended services towards her parent; and at the same time she gently deplored her own fate," Chapter Six

deplore:

express strong disapproval of

"...but her lessons were indelibly impressed on the mind of Safie, who sickened at the prospect of again returning to Asia and being immured within the walls of a harem, allowed only to occupy herself with infantile amusements," Chapter Six

immured:

closed in or confined

"The news reached Felix and roused him from his dream of pleasure. His blind and aged father and his gentle sister lay in a noisome dungeon while he enjoyed the free air and the society of her whom he loved," Chapter Six

noisome:

unpleasant in odor

"He could have endured poverty; and while this distress had been the meed of his virtue, he gloried in it," Chapter Seven

meed:

reward

"Besides, I found that my understanding improved so much with every day's experience that I was unwilling to commence this undertaking until a few more months should have added to my sagacity," Chapter Seven

sagacity:

having the qualities of wisdom

"I sat down, and a silence ensued. I knew that every minute was precious to me, yet I remained irresolute in what manner to commence the interview; when the old man addressed me," Chapter Seven

irresolute:

uncertain

"But on you only had I any claim for pity and redress," Chapter Eight

redress:

remedy, compensation

"The agony of my feelings allowed me no respite," Chapter Eight

respite:

a period of rest or relief

"The child still struggled, and loaded me with epithets which carried despair to my heart," Chapter Eight

epithet:

phrases of abuse

"I saw him descend the mountain with greater speed than the flight of an eagle, and quickly lost among the undulations of the sea of ice," Chapter Nine

undulations:

wavelike movements

Additional Homework

1. Ask students to prepare two thought questions of their own for a literature circle that they will facilitate in class, and which relate directly to a current global or local event.

Day 4 - Discussion of Thought Questions

1. What mixed signals does the creature get about humankind from the time he spends observing the cottagers?

Time:

10-15 min

Discussion:

Strong answers will observe examples that both reinforce the creature's anger towards people and redeem humankind despite his bad experiences. They should discuss the love of the cottagers for one another as the strongest proof that human are capable of good. This should also include reference to the embedded story about the merchant. In this, they should observe Felix as noble and loving and the merchant (as well as the society that imprisons him) as symbols of the darker sides of human nature. They should also look to the texts the creature finds as instructive and enlightening of both the triumphs and failures of human civilization. They may also consider his confusion about why they are so sad, despite the love they share.

2. What role does the creature's education play in his behavior and convictions?

Time:

10-15 min

Discussion:

Strong answers will show how his observations and readings informed his decisions and his general outlook on his life. They should discuss the creature's interpretation of those texts, and the way he puts them into the context of his own maltreatment by others. They should explain that by learning language, he gains the skills to reach out and communicate with others. They should find evidence of his acts of love (reaching out to others for companionship, gathering wood, saving a girl) and trace them back to examples of love and virtue in texts and in the behaviors of the cottagers. They should also explain how the evils he learns about and which recall his own condition (that he is more like Satan than Adam, for example) color his perception and help to justify his acts of violence against others.

3. Do you find the creature's responses to events fair or irrational and unjustified?

Time:

10-15 min

Discussion:

Strong answers should identify the more significant events of these chapters. These should include his decision to reach out to the family (and to the elder cottager specifically), to burn their house down when they reject him, to save the girl in the water, to take William's life and to implicate Justine in his murder. They should also consider his demand for a companion of his own as an important response to a long series of rejections and his painful isolation from others. They should discuss what reasons or causes are behind his behavior. In arguing whether or not the creature's isolation, rejection and suffering justifies his behavior, they should discuss whether or not these are the responses of a human being driven to extreme measures. In questioning who (if anyone else) is responsible for him, and what responsibility human beings have to one another, they may begin to question whether or not he is in fact human.

4. What is so tactful about the way the creature convinces Frankenstein to to help him?

Time:

10-15 min

Discussion:

Strong answers to this question should look closely at the creature's skillful use of the language as well as the sophistication of his argument over the course of his conversation. This should include a reference to Victor as both creator and father, and therefore the person responsible for his well-being. They should observe the way the creature manipulates Victor into feeling sympathy for him. They should refer to the story the creature tells as a method of evoking emotion.

5. What does the creature need in a companion, and do you think it would work out for him given the events so far?

Time:

10-15 min

Discussion:

Answers to the second part of the question will be subjective, but they should be based on their interpretation of the creature's need for a companion. They should summarize the creature's request and argument, observing instances of rejection by others, including Victor's own rejection, and the continual rejections thereafter (villagers, the cottagers, William). They should consider what the creature is really looking for, referring to some of the things he has learned from the texts he read as well. They may argue that he is really looking for a caretaker (the parent he never had) and that a companion fashioned in the same way would not exactly fulfill that request. They should discuss his need to be loved as well as any interest he has in actively loving someone else, which is something he would have to do as a companion. They may point to his acts of kindness as evidence that he could do that.

Day 4 - Short Answer Evaluation

1. What large city did the cottagers come from?

   _____

2. Name one fo the texts the creature was fortunate to find.

   _____

3. What did Felix offer the imprisoned Turk?

   _____

4. What did the imprisoned Turk offer Felix in return for his help?

   _____

5. Which of the cottagers did the creature decide to reach out to first?

   _____

6. What artifact of Victor's lab did the creature find in his possession?

   _____

7. How did the creature destroy the cottage?

   _____

8. Why was the creature shot at by a rustic in the woods?

   _____

9. What was the creatures request of Victor?

10. Why did Victror agree to satisfy the creature's request?

Answer Key

1. Paris.
2. Lives; Paradise Lost; Sorrows of Werter.
3. He offered to break him out and guide him to safetfy.
4. He said he would unite Felix with his daughter, Safie.
5. The elder cottager (De Lacey).
6. Victor's Journal.
7. He set it on fire.
8. He dragged a girl out of the water, and was assumed to be attacking her.
9. To make him a being just like him.
10. Victor was persuaded by his story; he felt responsible for the creature's misery and happiness.

Day 4 - Crossword Puzzle

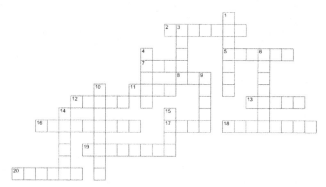

ACROSS

2. The creature went into the cottage and spoke to this man
5. The creature promised he would leave which continent forever?
7. In the texts the creature found, he learned about both good and _____
8. The creature longed for a companion, like this biblical figure
11. To Saifie, taking up residence in this Middle East country was an abhorrent idea
12. The creature found printed works consisting of bound pages, or these
13. The creature saw himself not as Adam, but as this fallen angel
16. De Lacey loathed the idea that his daughter would be with a _____
17. William called the creature an ___, the word for a man-eating giant
18. This Greek philosopher taught the creature high thoughts
19. Another word for Heaven, and the first word of a book the creature read
20. The creature felt as though he did not have a mother or a _____

DOWN

1. Another word for retribution
3. The creature descended the mountain with a speed greater than this regal bird
4. This person promised to get De Lacey out of prison
6. One who has been rejected from society is known as this
9. If you are away from and barred from your native country, you are in _____
10. A picture of a person, especially of the face, head and shoulders, or this
14. De Lacey was descended from a family in this country
15. The creature watched the family through this small opening

Crossword Puzzle Answer Key

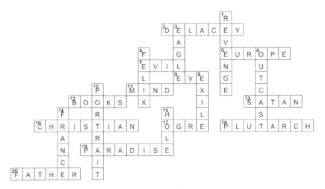

ACROSS

2. The creature went into the cottage and spoke to this man
5. The creature promised he would leave which continent forever?
7. In the texts the creature found, he learned about both good and _____
8. The creature longed for a companion, like this biblical figure
11. To Saifie, taking up residence in this Middle East country was an abhorrent idea
12. The creature found printed works consisting of bound pages, or these
13. The creature saw himself not as Adam, but as this fallen angel
16. De Lacey loathed the idea that his daughter would be with a _____
17. William called the creature an ___, the word for a man-eating giant
18. This Greek philosopher taught the creature high thoughts
19. Another word for Heaven, and the first word of a book the creature read
20. The creature felt as though he did not have a mother or a _____

DOWN

1. Another word for retribution
3. The creature descended the mountain with a speed greater than this regal bird
4. This person promised to get De Lacey out of prison
6. One who has been rejected from society is known as this
9. If you are away from and barred from your native country, you are in _____
10. A picture of a person, especially of the face, head and shoulders, or this
14. De Lacey was descended from a family in this country
15. The creature watched the family through this small opening

Day 4 - Vocabulary Quiz

Terms

1. _____ deplore
2. _____ immured
3. _____ noisome
4. _____ meed
5. _____ sagacity
6. _____ irresolute
7. _____ redress
8. _____ respite
9. _____ epithet
10. _____ undulations

Answers

A. phrases of abuse
B. wavelike movements
C. reward
D. uncertain
E. remedy, compensation
F. closed in or confined
G. a period of rest or relief
H. unpleasant in odor
I. having the qualities of wisdom
J. express strong disapproval of

Answer Key

1. J deplore: express strong disapproval of
2. F immured: closed in or confined
3. H noisome: unpleasant in odor
4. C meed: reward
5. I sagacity: having the qualities of wisdom
6. D irresolute: uncertain
7. E redress: remedy, compensation
8. G respite: a period of rest or relief
9. A epithet: phrases of abuse
10. B undulations: wavelike movements

Day 4 - Classroom Activities

1. Framed Narratives

Kind of Activity:

Individual Writing

Objective:

Students will be able to define the function of a literary device and interpret its effect on the reading.

Common Core Standards:

CCSS.ELA-Literacy.CCRA.SL.1

Time:

10-15 minutes (recurring)

Structure:

In this activity, students will discuss the meaning of a frame narrative and then include themselves in the frame by writing a letter to a friend about the story.

Have students define, discuss and share their own examples of frame narratives (or frame stories). Consider the following resource.

Ask students to discuss the following questions:

- What is the effect of a frame narrative?
- Why would an author use the device?
- How do the different narratives' themes relate to one another in *Frankenstein*?

Consider more interpretive questions:

- Do the frames make the story confusing?
- Did you feel more removed from the story with each shift in the frame?
- Did it seem like anything important was left behind?

Have students write a short synopsis of each narrative so far.

Ideas for Differentiated Instruction:

For visual learners, have students draw several boxes within one other. They may use sheets of paper, staggering them to create the impression of the frame within a frame. Have them write about each narrative, fixing them one within the other.

Assessment Ideas:

Finally, have the students write a very short letter to a friend or family explaining what they are reading in their class (Frankenstein) and what it is about. In their explanation of what it is about, have them focus on each of these narrators' stories (Walton's, Victor's, the creature's, the cottagers'). Discuss how they have created another frame around the whole story by writing a letter about the story.

2. Allusions

Kind of Activity:

Group Work

Objective:

Students will be able to analyse the significance of other texts or references in the story.

Common Core Standards:

CCSS.ELA-Literacy.CCRA.R.1, CCSS.ELA-Literacy.CCRA.R.2

Time:

50 min

Structure:

Have students interpret the significance of one of the allusions or references in the novel. Have them research the author and text, and then ask them to report on the way this allusion relates to (mirrors, contrasts, enhances) themes, conflicts motifs or events in the text.

Consider having students directly research the significance of these works and references in Frankenstein.

Consider the following list:

- The Legend of Prometheus
- One of the texts he found (*Plutarch's Lives*, *The Sorrows of Werter*, *Paradise Lost*, *Plutarch's Parallel Lives*, Goethe's *Sorrows of Young Werther*)
- Rime of the Ancient Mariner
- Fallen Angel (Satan)
- Adam

Ideas for Differentiated Instruction:

For students who struggle with independent research or who thrive in project-based activities, provide the option to attach this activity to the interview in this section. Have them (as the creature) explain a few things they learned about/from a text. In the case that it is a reference like the fallen angel, as them to explain how they feel like that individual.

Assessment Ideas:

Ask students to select a fact about/from their allusion/reference. Have them write a short refection on it and have them select a passage from the text that seems to capture its significance. Ask them to put these two texts side by side on a bulletin board or in a folder, and have them consider selecting images to accompany the document.

Day 5 - Reading Assignment, Questions, Vocabulary

Read **all chapters** in Volume 3. (This corresponds to **Chapters 18** through **24** in texts that do not use volumes).

Common Core Objectives

- CCSS.ELA-Literacy.CCRA.W.2 Write informative/explanatory texts to examine and convey complex ideas and information clearly and accurately through the effective selection, organization, and analysis of content.

- CCSS.ELA-Literacy.CCRA.R.7 Integrate and evaluate content presented in diverse media and formats, including visually and quantitatively, as well as in words.

Note that it is perfectly fine to expand any day's work into two days depending on the characteristics of the class, particularly if the class will engage in all of the suggested classroom exercises and activities and discuss all of the thought questions.

Content Summary for Teachers

All Chapters of Volume 3

Chapter 1

Victor returns home, torn about his decision to help the creature. He becomes dismayed and morose over the realization that it will require a great deal of work. Feeling the comforts of home, he delays getting started, and all but forgets about the task. He will marry Elizabeth, but he does not want to marry her without completing the job, so he vows to marry her when he returns from England, where he must go to research and begin his work. Clerval accompanies Victor, and Victor also realizes that the creature will be following him on the journey. He is tormented by the idea of the creature, who follows him, but he realizes it's better than if the creature stalked his family in Geneva. They travel through Europe to London. The journey reveals the diverging preoccupations of the two friends — Victor in a state of angst over the reality of his journey, and Clerval eager to continue his studies.

Chapter 2

Clerval and Victor set up in London, where Clerval partakes in the pleasures of studying abroad, and where Victor remains stifled and preoccupied with the daunting task of getting his experiments underway. The two of them set out for Scotland after receiving a letter to visit an acquaintance there, stopping in university towns along the way. Victor recalls his love for nature, the landscape of the north reminding him of home. Victor keeps an eye on Henry, worried the monster will come after him. Victor decides to work at an even more remote place in the countryside to make progress on his experiments. He remains torn about his work, delaying it further, concerned about the action the creature will take if he does not follow through on it.

Chapter 3

Inside his lab at night, and fearing the consequences of making another monster, Victor observes the creature watching him and destroys what he has so far created. The creature visits him later, threatening to wreak havoc on him for not following through with his promise. After receiving a letter from Henry asking him to rendezvous in Perth and return south with him again, he boards a small boat and disposes of the remains of his experiments. He falls asleep in the boat and awakes in treacherous waters, only to finally find his way to shore. Ashore, he meets with a crowd of people who suspect him of murder, and he goes away with the magistrate.

Chapter 4

The magistrate tells him that a man has been murdered near the site of Victor's arrival. Because of the age of the deceased and the manner in which he had been killed, Victor fears for the worst, and eventually finds that it is indeed Henry. Victor breaks down and is carried away. Victor remains bedridden for two months. The magistrate, Mr. Kirwin, is the only one to treat him kindly during this time, having come across Victor's papers and realizing the true nature of events. Kirwin also brings in the elder Frankenstein to visit Victor. Although Victor feels (ironically) as though he is doomed to remain alive through all of this tragedy, his father's presence calms him temporarily. They plan their journey back to Geneva.

Chapter 5

They stop in Paris along the way home. Victor shares his confused emotions with his father, who believes that Victor's extreme guilt is a result of his grief. He receives a letter from Elizabeth, who expresses her concern that Victor may not want to marry her. He vows to marry her when he returns. He is happy to be reunited with Elizabeth, and he tells her that he will explain the reasons for his misery after they get married. But he is constantly cautious, carrying a pistol everywhere he goes. Victor's father wonders if Victor's unrelenting anxiety is a matter of his marriage to Elizabeth, but Victor assures him that this is not the case. The two marry and journey to a villa on the shores of Lake Como — an estate that Elizabeth inherited and the site of their honeymoon. Although Elizabeth makes an effort to appease Victor along the way, a dark cloud seems to hang over both of them.

Chapter 6

At Como, Elizabeth asks what plagues Victor, but he cannot bring himself to tell her. Victor tells Elizabeth to relax in bed, and he paces the house, armed with a pistol and worried about when and where the creature might strike. After hearing a scream, he runs to the bedroom and finds Elizabeth strangled and dead. He collapses out of grief and awakes to see the creature looking through the window. Victor fires his pistol at him, and begs others to pursue the murderer. In anguish, Victor returns to Geneva to make sure his father and Ernest are safe. He finds them safe and at home. However, his father does not handle the news well, and he soon dies. Victor is put into an asylum. After resting and coming to his senses, he finds the town magistrate and discloses everything, but the magistrate is skeptical and decides not to follow up on Victor's potential delusions. Victor decides to hunt the creature down on his own.

Chapter 7

Victor visits the cemetery where his family is buried, and then he leaves the country, taking what money he has along with some of his mother's jewelry. He explains to Walton that he followed the creature over great distances, aided by people who spoke of his presence and by messages and marks the creature left behind to help Victor pursue him. Both the creature and Victor acquire sledges to travel over the treacherous territory of the north. Finally in the north and over stretches of ice, he glimpses the creature in the distance. Shortly thereafter, the ice breaks up and Victor becomes stranded on a single ice flow. Resigned to death, he catches sight of Walton's ship, takes to the water and paddles out to him. Here, we are caught up to the present in the narration.

Victor, barely alive, begs Walton to pursue the creature if he dies. On the brink of a mutiny, the sailors ask Walton to head south after the ice breaks up, instead of continuing on their journey. Unsure of what to do, and after continued requests by Victor to pursue the creature — appealing to Walton's sense of desire and adventure — Walton decides that he will indeed return home. Dismayed by Walton's decision, Victor passes away.

That evening, upon hearing a noise in the chamber where Victor lies, Walton arrives to find the creature hanging over his creator, lamenting his death. Walton is at the same time in awe of the creature and condemnatory of his crimes. The creature addresses the crimes others committed against him, but ultimately vows to rid the earth of his rage, and to take his own life. The creature disappears.

Thought Questions (students consider while they read)

1. Why doesn't Victor tell anyone in his family about the creature's threat to them, and what does this say about his character?

2. What joys or interests does Victor's increasing fear and obsession destroy and prevent him from sharing with others?

3. Why does Victor destroy the creature's potential companion?

4. Victor explains to Walton that he had lost his capacity for voluntary thought. What are some examples supporting this reflection, and what were some early signs of this problem?

5. How does Walton seem to learn from Frankenstein's narrative, even despite some of Frankenstein's conflicting messages?

Vocabulary (in order of appearance)

"It had been her care which provided me a companion in Clerval – and yet a man is blind to a thousand minute circumstances, which call forth a woman's sedulous attention," Chapter One

sedulous:

showing hard work and dedication

"I looked towards its completion with a tremulous and eager hope, which I dared not trust myself to question, but which was intermixed with obscure forebodings of evil, that made my heart sicken in my bosom," Chapter Two

tremulous:

shaking nervously

"I left the house, the horrid scene of the last night's contention, and walked on the beach of the sea, which I almost regarded as an insuperable barrier between me and my fellow-creatures," Chapter Three

insuperable:

difficult or impossible to defeat or overcome

"Little did I then expect the calamity that was in a few moments to overwhelm me, and extinguish in horror and despair all fear of ignominy or death," Chapter Three

ignominy:

shame or disgrace

"The magistrate observed me with a keen eye, and of course drew an unfavourable augury from my manner," Chapter Four

augury:

an omen or a sign; the work of one who performs augurs

"...but he did not know the origin of my sufferings, and sought erroneous methods to remedy the incurable ill," Chapter FIve

erroneous :

incorrect

"My father was in the mean time overjoyed, and in the bustle of preparation only recognised in the melancholy of his niece the diffidence of a bride," Chapter Five

diffidence:

shyness or modesty

"We walked for a short time on the shore, enjoying the transitory light, and then retired to the inn," Chapter Six

transitory:

always changing or moving; not permanent

"Amidst the wilds of Tartary and Russia, although he still evaded me, I have ever followed in his track. Sometimes the peasants, scared by this horrid apparition," Chapter Seven

apparition:

the ghost-like appearance of someone or something

"Why do you not hate Felix, who drove his friend from the door with contumely?" Chapter Seven

contumely:

insulting treatment

Additional Homework

1. Have students investigate the role between creator and creation. Explain that this is intentionally vague to support many kinds of creators (artists across media, engineers, mythological figures, a mother) and their creations. Have them select one of these which they find compelling, and to bring into class a written refection on what they found out. Ask them to consider examples across culture, history and forms.

Day 5 - Discussion of Thought Questions

1. Why doesn't Victor tell anyone in his family about the creature's threat to them, and what does this say about his character?

Time:

10-15 min

Discussion:

Interpretations will be subjective, but strong answers will reference Victor's patterns and motivations throughout the story. They may discuss how his reasons for keeping the secret are rooted in a complex character flaw. They should consider his habit of studying in isolation, hiding his research and experiments from the beginning. They should also consider the fact that he regretted his creation from the moment it came into being, and that he was ashamed of it. They should discuss why. They should consider if and how he realized that he was misguided by obsession, and how that led to the deaths for which he feels responsible. They may also discuss his fear that they would consider him crazy.

2. What joys or interests does Victor's increasing fear and obsession destroy and prevent him from sharing with others?

Time:

10-15 min

Discussion:

Strong answers will observe Victor's healthier interests and passions, and those of the loved ones around him with whom he is involved. These should include his love of nature, which he is aware of but cannot relish in along his journeys to England and

Scotland. They should discuss Henry's appreciation for the gems of nature along the river, and his excitement about studying in England and traveling to India as things he might have also enjoyed. They should consider Elizabeth's love as something impossible for him to revel in.

3. Why does Victor destroy the creature's potential companion?

Time:

10-15 min

Discussion:

Strong answers will go beyond the objections Victor originally had to designing another creature. They should observe his reflections on the potential horrors of this second creature's existence. These include his fear that they would have offspring and make way for an entire race, the potential for them to dislike or become repulsed by one another and his worry that they would simply commit further atrocities together. They may also observe that he began destroying his second experiment while the creature was observing him; they may consider the significance of the timing there. More subjective interpretations may look deeper into the symbolism of his dysfunctional relationship with the creature. They may explore his role as parent (father and/or mother) or even as a kind of companion.

4. Victor explains to Walton that he had lost his capacity for voluntary thought. What are some examples supporting this reflection, and what were some early signs of this problem?

Time:

10-15 min

Discussion:

Strong answers will observe the fact that he doesn't warn his family about the creature's threat or tell them anything about the specific details surrounding its tragedies. He doesn't enlist Clerval more fully in his affairs, he doesn't take the life of the creature when he has the chance and he vows to marry Elizabeth knowing the threat the creature poses. They should discuss the fact that he suffers from obsessive fears and worries but continues to put himself and everyone around him in danger. They may discuss his inability to enjoy anything he showed previous interest in, and they may point to his obsessions early on (from studying in isolation to becoming sick throughout the creation of the creature) as signs that he was losing control of his thoughts earlier.

5. How does Walton seem to learn from Frankenstein's narrative, even despite some of Frankenstein's conflicting messages?

Time:

10-15 min

Discussion:

Students should discuss Walton's decision to return southward when the ice breaks up, observing the relationship of this decision to Victor's warnings of pursuing a lust for power and fame. They should observe Walton's loyalty to his men as a contrast to Victor's failure to protect his family. Students should also refer to the conversation Walton has with the creature in the ship, discussing Walton's logical and sober thoughts regarding the creature's deeds. They may also observe that Walton showed no interest in destroying the creature — the compulsion which finally drove Frankenstein into madness. Discussions may reflect on the fact that he warns Walton to temper his thirst for discovery at the same time as he tries to encourage his pursuit of the creature.

Day 5 - Short Answer Evaluation

1. Why didn't Vicror want to marry Elizabeth immediately?

   _____

2. Where did Victor resolve to go in order to begin his research and work for the new creature?

   _____

3. What horrible result did Victor imagine could come of his two creature's coming together?

   _____

4. What did they find along the neck of Clerval when they first inspeted him?

   _____

5. How did Mr. Kirwin discover the truth of the events?

   _____

6. Who came to see Victor in the prison?

   _____

7. To whom did Victor finally reveal the truth of the creature?

   _____

8. What did the creature do to help Victor follow him?

   _____

9. What does Victor ask Walton to do if he dies?

_____

10. What did the sailors ask Walton to promise them when the ice shifted?

_____

Answer Key

1. He couldn't marry her with his unfinished task looming over him and his family.
2. England.
3. He imagined them having children; he imagined them hating each other; he imagined them committing more crimes.
4. The black marks of the creatures fingers.
5. He found Victor's papers.
6. His father.
7. The magistrate in Geneva.
8. He left marks and messages.
9. To pursue and kill the creature.
10. They asked him to turn around and go south (home).

Day 5 - Crossword Puzzle

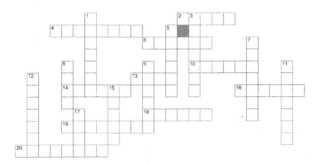

ACROSS

2. The creature said that he would turn his body to cinders, or these

4. Frankenstein feared that he would be driven into the open waters of this ocean

6. Mr. _____, or the magistrate

10. Frankenstein and Clerval stopped in this college town on the way to Scotland

13. These animals accompanied the creature and Frankenstein on their chase

14. The creature evaded Frankenstein throughout this large country of the east

16. Frankenstein carried a handgun, also called this

18. Both the creature and Frankenstein acquired this vehicle for moving over ice

19. The elder Frankenstein anticipated the _____ of his son with Elizabeth

20. Frankenstein entered this final resting place to visit his family's graves

DOWN

1. Frankenstein and Clerval saw many ruins of these magnificent buildings

3. These seafaring men asked Walton to head south after the ice broke

5. Frankenstein returned to see if his father and _____ were still alive

7. The creature said, "I will be with you on your _____ night"

8. This outer surface of the tree in which the creature left writings

9. The word for a dead body, especially of a human being

11. Frankenstein was not rushing to fulfill his _____ to the creature

12. Another word for fairness or equity, which the creature longed for

15. Clerval would discuss his desire to travel to this Asian country

17. Elizabeth had a villa on a body of water, which is also called this

Crossword Puzzle Answer Key

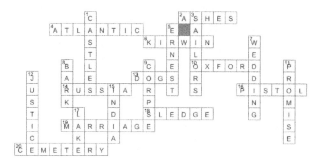

ACROSS

2. The creature said that he would turn his body to cinders, or these
4. Frankenstein feared that he would be driven into the open waters of this ocean
6. Mr. _____, or the magistrate
10. Frankenstein and Clerval stopped in this college town on the way to Scotland
13. These animals accompanied the creature and Frankenstein on their chase
14. The creature evaded Frankenstein throughout this large country of the east
16. Frankenstein carried a handgun, also called this
18. Both the creature and Frankenstein acquired this vehicle for moving over ice
19. The elder Frankenstein anticipated the _____ of his son with Elizabeth
20. Frankenstein entered this final resting place to visit his family's graves

DOWN

1. Frankenstein and Clerval saw many ruins of these magnificent buildings
3. These seafaring men asked Walton to head south after the ice broke
5. Frankenstein returned to see if his father and _____ were still alive
7. The creature said, "I will be with you on your _____ night"
8. This outer surface of the tree in which the creature left writings
9. The word for a dead body, especially of a human being
11. Frankenstein was not rushing to fulfill his _____ to the creature
12. Another word for fairness or equity, which the creature longed for
15. Clerval would discuss his desire to travel to this Asian country
17. Elizabeth had a villa on a body of water, which is also called this

Day 5 - Vocabulary Quiz

Terms

1. _____ sedulous
2. _____ tremulous
3. _____ insuperable
4. _____ ignominy
5. _____ augury
6. _____ erroneous
7. _____ diffidence
8. _____ transitory
9. _____ apparition
10. _____ contumely

Answers

A. shame or disgrace
B. insulting treatment
C. incorrect
D. difficult or impossible to defeat or overcome
E. shyness or modesty
F. always changing or moving; not permanent
G. shaking nervously
H. showing hard work and dedication
I. the ghost-like appearance of someone or something
J. an omen or a sign; the work of one who performs augurs

Answer Key

1. H sedulous: showing hard work and dedication
2. G tremulous: shaking nervously
3. D insuperable: difficult or impossible to defeat or overcome
4. A ignominy: shame or disgrace
5. J augury: an omen or a sign; the work of one who performs augurs
6. C erroneous : incorrect
7. E diffidence: shyness or modesty
8. F transitory: always changing or moving; not permanent
9. I apparition: the ghost-like appearance of someone or something
10. B contumely: insulting treatment

Day 5 - Classroom Activities

1. Visual Art

Kind of Activity:

Creative Writing

Objective:

Students will show their understanding of the text's historical and cultural context.

Common Core Standards:

CCSS.ELA-Literacy.CCRA.R.7

Time:

50 min

Structure:

In this activity, students will relate evidence of Romantic themes in the text to those same themes in visual art.

Ask students to explore the tenets of Romanticism as they relate to both literature and visual art.

Have students select a number of passages in volume 2 which they believe represent those Romantic ideals. Have students look at three aspects of the text and of the art they choose:

1. Content: What the author/artist chooses to deal with.
2. Theme: Messages and philosophies expressed by the work.
3. Form: The style of the work itself.

After students select 2-3 works of art, use Visual Thinking Strategies as will as more prescriptive methods to help them begin their analysis.

Ideas for Differentiated Instruction:

Ask students who struggle to identify abstract themes in the writing to select paintings which would serve as appropriate color plates for the text. Have them pair these pictures with their complimentary passages.

Assessment Ideas:

Ask students to display their chosen works of art, and to informally talk on the qualities of the connections they found to *Frankenstein*.

2. Story Shape

Kind of Activity:

Group Discussion

Objective:

Students will be able to analyze the intersection of character development and plot.

Common Core Standards:

CCSS.ELA-Literacy.CCRA.W.2

Time:

50 min

Structure:

Discussion: Have students explore Kurt Vonnegut's charts about the shapes of stories. Discuss the different shapes and have students share the shapes of other stories they like.

Ask students to choose or design the shape that best suits *Frankenstein*. Have them mark plot events on the chart. As they do this, and with the idea of a the frame narrative from a previous activity in mind, ask students to choose a shape that best suits each narrative in the story. Remember to have them consider that each shape is within the one that precedes it.

Discussion: Also ask students to identify who (what character) drives the shape of the story. Interpretations here will vary, and multiple character may play more or less of a role in driving the shape of the story.

Ideas for Differentiated Instruction:

For students who struggle to see how the charts relate to the story, consider the option to create a diagram for the story where the x-axis is time, and the y-axis is tension, as at the following source.

Assessment Ideas:

To extend the activity, ask students to consider what would have to happen in the story to make it fit one of the other charts, or to change its shape to suit their wishes for the characters in the story.

Final Paper

Essay Questions

1. Analyze the structure of the text, and discuss which part of the story's structure evokes the most criticism.

2. Should the creature be taken for a complete human being, and if so, should he be held responsible for his actions? Discuss the factors which played a role in his development as an individual and ultimately in his behavior.

3. Explain the unique relationship between isolation and achievement in each narrative in the story.

4. Is this a novel about failure, and what lessons are we to learn from the characters' endeavors?

5. Describe the significance of the story's structure, and discuss how this structure mirrors its central characters' ordeals.

6. How are the female characters depicted by the narrators of the story?

7. In what ways is *Frankenstein* a work of Romantic literature, and which Romantic ideal is the most prominent in Victor Frankenstein's character?

Advice on research sources

A. School or community library

Ask your reference librarian for help locating books on the following subjects:

- Romanticism (and all subcategories)
- Science in Literature
- Mary Shelley
- 18th and 19th Century novelists
- (Also consider researching the themes discussed in this guide.)

B. Personal Experience

Ask students to reflect on their own experience with the themes discussed in this guide (free will, responsibility, the thirst for power).

Grading rubric for essays

Style:

- Words: word choice, spelling, and diction
- Sentences: grammar and punctuation
- Paragraphs: organization, topic sentences, and supporting sentences
- Essay: opening argument or statement of opinion, paragraphs, and conclusion
- Argument: strength, analysis, and creativity

Students may use The Elements of Style as a resource.

Content:

- Use of evidence from the text and accuracy of subject matter
- Addressing complex and sensitive subjects with understanding and nuance
- Addressing and resolving raised questions
- Use of literary concepts

Students may use Harvard Writing Center's resources on essays to support their writing

Answer Key for Final Essays

Remember that essays about literature should not be graded with a cookie-cutter approach whereby specific words or ideas are required. See the grading rubric above for a variety of criteria to use in assessing answers to the essay questions. This answer key thus functions as a store of ideas for students who need additional guidance in framing their answers.

1. Analyze the structure of the text, and discuss which part of the story's structure evokes the most criticism.

Students should choose a point in (or aspect of) the plot to bring under a critical lens. This paper is meant to give students an entry point into an analysis of the writing (rather than character or theme), though they should discuss character and theme in their critique. Papers should elaborate on the structure of the story, defining it and identifying aspects of it which seem weak, questionable, overly complex, or which they simply feel critical of. There are several aspects of the plot which are popularly criticized or questioned, and students may decide to discuss one that came up throughout their own discussion of the text. This may have arisen as a complaint. For example, students may decide to critique why Shelley had the creature walk out of the lab and disappear. They may have found it odd that Victor simply seemed to say,

"OK, he's gone. Phew!" They might explain that it was unlikely that the creature would not have been discovered by the cottagers. They may find the ending anticlimactic or enigmatic. Whichever point in the plot they choose, they should critique the choices of the author.

2. Should the creature be taken for a complete human being, and if so, should he be held responsible for his actions? Discuss the factors which played a role in his development as an individual and ultimately in his behavior.

In this question, students should explore the themes of determinism and free will in the novel, considering his nature and nurture in his development as a character. They should discuss the influences of the world around the creature. These include his experiences, his relationships and his learning through reading and by observation. They should include an analysis of his observation of the cottagers, discussing *what* and especially *how* he learns from them. They should include an analysis of the texts he reads and hears read aloud, considering the direct effect these stories and histories had on his thinking and behavior. They may discuss whether there was anything about his biology that defines his specific behavior or the way he is treated by others. They may look at his own experience surviving alone in nature, where he lacked socialization. They should also consider the impact of being abandoned on his development. They should discuss the totality of these factors and how (or if) they should make him as accountable as anyone else.

3. Explain the unique relationship between isolation and achievement in each narrative in the story.

Papers should begin by defining this relationship. For example, they may argue that great achievement leads one to a place or phase of isolation for significant reasons. They should begin with Walton's narrative and the setting of the stranded ship in an already very isolated part of the world. They should describe Walton's longing for a companion. They should discuss the way Frankenstein separates himself from others early on and especially at the height of his experiments throughout the novel. They should look at the periods when he isolated himself in the mountains. They will consider the creature's own isolation in nature and separation from others, and his desire to be part of society in contrast to that. They should consider what insights and realizations these characters have in their isolation. They may also discuss the isolation of De Lacey in prison, and then the isolation of the cottagers, even if they have each other.

4. Is this a novel about failure, and what lessons are we to learn from the characters' endeavors?

Papers should explore the three narrators' endeavors, and they should also consider the story of the cottagers as a smaller narrative reflecting this theme. They should relate the lesson of each failure to the whole argument. Papers should look at Walton's experience as a kind of failure which sets the stage (quite literally) for the other narratives. They should look closely at Victor's trials and errors, considering that though he succeeded in creating an individual, he rarely reflects on his condition as anything but increasingly miserable. They will look at the creature's experience as one fraught with failure (the failure to make acquaintances, to become part of a family, to gain the acceptance of his creator). They may also consider the failure of the cottagers to thrive on their own. Papers should identify a unique interpretation of the overall lesson from these failures. They may argue, for example, that while one's lust for power could be successful, it would ultimately lead to ruin. They could consider this a lesson Walton did not have to learn on his own, and they may consider this his ultimate discovery, making his journey a kind of success.

5. Describe the significance of the story's structure, and discuss how this structure mirrors its central characters' ordeals.

Papers should define *frame narrative*, and provide a strong description of the narratives that make up the story, identifying themes they share and which they believe relate to the structure of the work as a whole. They should include *creation* among them. Most notably, they should discuss the fact that the creature is made up of the parts of deceased people, much like the text is made up of the voices of different narrators. They should look deeper into this recursive quality, finding things about the creature which relate back to the way the story is told. They should discuss the fact that although the narratives can be separated, they are bound together by their storytellers, the one's who bring them into existence. They may also explore that fact that each character gets a chance to narrate — to speak in the first person — reflecting their place at what they feel is the center of the story.

6. How are the female characters depicted by the narrators of the story?

Papers might begin by noting that there are no female narrators, and that all we know of them is related secondhand, reflecting a more passive role in the story, despite their significance to the narrators. They may argue that this reflects their passive but central role in some of the narrator's lives (as objects of affection, as primary caretakers, or as the objects of revenge, for example). It should also be observed that Safie is discussed through the creature's lenses. Papers should look closely at the tone, mood and material of Walton's letters to his sister. They should observe the way

Victor discusses his mother and the significance of his mother and his cousin to his story about himself early on and throughout his narrative. They should consider the creature's observations and his request for a female companion, and they should interpret this request in light of what the creature has learned and observed about men and women. They should focus closely on Victor's destruction of the female creation, and on his relationship (and more importantly his reflections on) Elizabeth at this time and up to the point of her death. Students may notice that there is little dialogue between women, noting the narrators' tendencies to discuss female characters in relation to themselves only.

7. In what ways is *Frankenstein* a work of Romantic literature, and which Romantic ideal is the most prominent in Victor Frankenstein's character?

Papers should identify the tenets or ideals that are central to Romanticism. They should show how the novel reflects several of these before they set into their specific focus on Victor Frankenstein. They should focus on an element of Romanticism which includes the main action and tension in the novel, and which is present in each of the narratives (Walton's, Victor's and the creatures), even if it focuses mostly on Victor Frankenstein himself. They may focus on the deep sense of or awareness of the individual as situated in the natural world, on the individual's passionate fulfillment of an emotional need or on the attainment of something greater than ordinary human achievement.

Final Exam

Multiple Choice

Circle the letter corresponding to the best answer.

1. What is the name of the university Victor Frankenstein attends?

    A. University of Vienna
    B. The Austrian College of Sciences
    C. Geneva College
    D. University of Ingolstadt

2. Frankenstein is held as an example of one of the first of this type of story:

    A. Epic Poetry
    B. Romance
    C. Children's
    D. Science Fiction

3. Who of the following was murdered by the monster?

    A. Clerval
    B. Caroline
    C. Margaret
    D. Walton

4. Who are the story's three main narrators?

    A. Walton and Clerval
    B. Walton, Victor, the Monster
    C. Walton and the Monster
    D. Victor and Clerval

5. Which of these locations is NOT a setting for the story's events?

    A. Geneva

B. Spain
C. Archangel
D. The Arctic Circle

6. Who is a famous poet quoted within the novel?

A. Samuel Taylor Coleridge
B. Homer
C. Lord Byron
D. Percy Shelley

7. Where does the Monster promise to go if Frankenstein creates a mate for him?

A. Switzerland
B. Siberia
C. St. Petersburg
D. South America

8. Two characters in the story directly compare themselves to this biblical figure:

A. Isaac
B. Abraham
C. Ishmael
D. Adam

9. Who was the monster's first victim?

A. Alphonse
B. William
C. Felix
D. Justine

10. In a letter at the start of the book, Walton alludes to a poem by saying he will not kill this bird:

A. Snow Owl
B. Seagull
C. Albatross
D. Kingfisher

11. What book does the monster read causing him to speculate about his role in existence:

A. Prometheus Bound
B. Paradise Lost
C. The Bible
D. The Ancient Mariner

12. What is the name of the family the Monster stalks and tries to communicate with?

A. Clerval
B. De Lacey
C. Walton
D. Moritz

13. Who is falsely accused of being Clerval's murderer?

A. Victor
B. Justine Moritz
C. Walton
D. Alphonse

14. What does Victor's father reproach him for reading?

A. Agrippa
B. Homer
C. Paradise Lost
D. Chemistry textbooks

15. The monster stops stealing food from the cottagers once he notices their:

A. Servants
B. Poverty
C. Sickly livestock
D. Religion

16. Which of these characters is present in Victor's childhood?

A. Margaret

B. Clerval
C. Krempe
D. Walton

17. Elizabeth, Victor's betrothed, is also his:

A. Neighbor
B. Niece
C. Cousin
D. Sister

18. Who does Walton compare himself to in his journey north?

A. his father
B. the Monster
C. The Great Poets
D. Marco Polo

19. In what form is this novel written?

A. Omniscient point of view
B. Epistolary
C. Play
D. Stream of consciousness

20. Who does Walton encounter in his cabin at the end of the novel?

A. Margaret
B. The monster
C. Frankenstein
D. A ghost of Victor

Short Answer

1. Who are the three main narrators in the text?

   _____

2. How do the three of the main narrators in the text wind up in the same place (in the north)?

   _____

3. Who does the creature kill with his own hands?

   _____

4. What did Justine give William which later made her feel guilty about his death?

   _____

5. Where was the De Lacey cottage?

   _____

6. To which Biblical figures does the creature continually compare himself?

   _____

7. Who did the creature call his "protectors"?

   _____

8. Where did Elizabeth and Victor go after their marriage?

   _____

9. How did Victor's father die?

10. How does the creature say he will die?

Vocabulary Questions

Terms

1. _____ fervant
2. _____ chimerical
3. _____ abstruse
4. _____ indefatigable
5. _____ languor
6. _____ noisome
7. _____ odious
8. _____ timorous
9. _____ sullen
10. _____ impervious
11. _____ deplore
12. _____ insuperable

Answers

A. unable to be stopped
B. incapable of being penetrated
C. a state of fatigue
D. difficult to understand
E. intensely passionate
F. difficult or impossible to defeat or overcome
G. very unpleasant
H. imaginary or unreal
I. having a terrible odor
J. fear from lack of confidence
K. express strong disapproval of
L. depressive, sad

Short Essays

1. Explain Victor's aversion to the creature as a product of his difficulty with relationships in general.

_____

_____

_____

_____

_____

2. Do the characters in the story travel great distances by choice or are they compelled to do so? What is the significance of the characters' journeys over land and water throughout the story?

_____

_____

_____

_____

_____

3. Which characters undergo the greatest changes in the novel, and what sets
    their changes in motion?

_____

_____

_____

_____

Final Exam Answer Key

Multiple Choice

1. **(D)** University of Ingolstadt
2. **(D)** Science Fiction
3. **(A)** Clerval
4. **(B)** Walton, Victor, the Monster
5. **(B)** Spain
6. **(A)** Samuel Taylor Coleridge
7. **(D)** South America
8. **(D)** Adam
9. **(B)** William
10. **(C)** Albatross
11. **(B)** Paradise Lost
12. **(C)** Walton
13. **(A)** Victor
14. **(A)** Agrippa
15. **(B)** Poverty
16. **(B)** Clerval
17. **(C)** Cousin
18. **(C)** The Great Poets
19. **(B)** Epistolary
20. **(B)** The monster

Short Answer

1. Walton, Frankenstein and the creature.
2. Walton is searching for a passage to the North Pole. Victor Frankenstein is chasing the creature, who has fled north on a sledge.
3. William, Clerval and Elizabeth.
4. The locket with the picture of Caroline.
5. In the woods in Germany.
6. The fallen angel; Satan; sometimes Adam.
7. The cottagers; the De Lacey family.
8. Lake Como in Italy; To Elizabeth's inheritance Villa Lavenza.
9. He could not survive the grief after hearing of Elizabeth's death.
10. He says that he will "ascend his own funeral pile triumphantly, and exult in the agony of the torturing flames," therefore taking his own life.

Vocabulary Questions

1. E fervant: intensely passionate
2. H chimerical: imaginary or unreal
3. D abstruse: difficult to understand
4. A indefatigable : unable to be stopped
5. C languor: a state of fatigue
6. I noisome : having a terrible odor
7. G odious: very unpleasant
8. J timorous: fear from lack of confidence
9. L sullen: depressive, sad
10. B impervious: incapable of being penetrated
11. K deplore: express strong disapproval of
12. F insuperable: difficult or impossible to defeat or overcome

Short Essays

1. Essays should analyze the nature of his relationships early on, looking for signs of behavior that would make for unhealthy or confused relations later. They should observe the significance of Victor's relationship with his parents, with Clerval and Elizabeth as a child and then later as an adult, with his professors and finally with the creature. They should also note that all we learn about his relationships comes directly from him. They may consider how his seemingly justifiable reasons for fading away from Elizabeth revealed themselves much earlier in his life (when he isolated himself to quench his thirst for knowledge, and when he failed to write letters home). They may question his devotion to Elizabeth — a woman he grew up with as a cousin (but someone he saw as a sister). They may also discuss his inability to define what his relationship to the creature should be (father, mother, brother, or something else). Essays may acknowledge other reasons for his aversion to his creation, explaining that some other underlying interpersonal issue is playing a significant role in his tragic rejection of the creature.

2. Essays should explore the reasons for characters' journeys over the course of the narratives. As with many discussions and essays regarding this text, it may help for students to structure their response in a way that reflects the frames of the story, looking at Walton, then Victor and the creature, and even the journey of the cottagers. They should find connections (or a similar theme) in characters' travels. This could be a deep thirst for belonging, for power, for meaning, or even escape. It should be noted that Walton's ship is stuck, his paused journey framing all of the others. They should discuss the way Victor's and Clerval's research continually takes them away from home or from others, just as Walton's must have. They should discuss anything the characters might reflect on along their travels

(such as nature or their longing for others), and they should discuss the creature's reasons for moving such long distances (revenge, survival, belonging). They should finally be sure to argue how much of characters' movement across Europe and beyond is a matter of free will, or whether they are compelled to move by something out of their control.

3. Essays will identify at least one character, but they may discuss several. These should certainly include the creature and Victor. They may also observe Elizabeth's development from optimist to cynic. They may look at the entire Frankenstein family as one that takes on a similar kind of change, Victor himself embodying the most drastic form of this change from light to dark. They should observe the creature's growth and development as unique in that he develops knowledge and understanding but remains emotionally stunted by his lack of human contact. They should observe Victor's thirst for power and his lust after knowledge as the motivating force behind such developments, and they may look at Walton as a character who is spared such tragic changes, but one who becomes more level-headed in the end.

Lesson Plans

GradeSaver™

Getting you the grade since 1999™

Other Lesson Plans from GradeSaver™

12 Angry Men
1984
A Christmas Carol
A Doll's House
A Farewell to Arms
Alexander Hamilton
Alice in Wonderland
Allen Ginsberg's
   Poetry
All Quiet on the
   Western Front
All the Light We
   Cannot See
Americanah
Angela's Ashes
Animal Farm
An Inspector Calls
Anna Karenina
Antigone
A Passage to India
A Raisin in the Sun
Arcadia

Around the World in
   80 Days
A Separate Peace
As I Lay Dying
A Streetcar Named
   Desire
A Tale of Two Cities
A Thousand
   Splendid Suns
Atonement
A View From the
   Bridge
Beloved
Beowulf
Between the World
   and Me
Bhagavad-Gita
Black Boy
Bless Me, Ultima
Brave New World
Breakfast at
   Tiffany's

Bury My Heart at
   Wounded Knee
Call of the Wild
Cannery Row
Catching Fire
Cathedral
Cat's Cradle
Ceremony
Christopher
   Marlowe's Poems
Connecticut Yankee
   in King Arthur's
   Court
Death of a Salesman
Desire Under the
   Elms
Do Androids Dream
   of Electric Sheep?
Doctor Faustus
   (Marlowe)
Dr. Jekyll and Mr.
   Hyde
Dubliners

GradeSaver™

Getting you the grade since 1999™

Other Lesson Plans from GradeSaver™

Emily Dickinson's
  Collected Poems
Emma
Ender's Game
Equus
Esperanza Rising
Everyman: Morality
  Play
Fahrenheit 451
Fangirl
Fear and Loathing in
  Las Vegas
Flannery O'Connor's
  Stories
Flowers for
  Algernon
For Colored Girls
  Who Have
  Considered
  Suicide When the
  Rainbow Is Enuf
Founding Brothers
Frankenstein

Franny and Zooey
Gone Girl
Go Set a Watchman
Go Tell it On the
  Mountain
Great Expectations
Gulliver's Travels
Hamlet
Hatchet
Heart of Darkness
Holes
House of Mirth
House on Mango
  Street
How the Garcia
  Girls Lost Their
  Accents
I Am Malala
I Know Why the
  Caged Bird Sings
Incidents in the Life
  of a Slave Girl
In Cold Blood

In the Time of the
  Butterflies
Into the Wild
Into Thin Air
Invisible Man
Island of the Blue
  Dolphins
Jane Eyre
John Donne: Poems
Jorge Borges: Short
  Stories
Journey to the
  Center of the
  Earth
Julius Caesar
Juno and the
  Paycock
Kate Chopin's Short
  Stories
Kindred
King Lear
Last of the
  Mohicans

For our full list of over 300 Study Guides, Quizzes, Lesson Plans
Sample College Application Essays, Literature Essays and E-texts, visit:

www.gradesaver.com

Lesson Plans

GradeSaver™

Getting you the grade since 1999™

Other Lesson Plans from GradeSaver™

Leaves of Grass
Let the Circle be
  Unbroken
Life of Pi
Little Women
Looking for Alaska
Lord Byron's Poems
Lord Jim
Lord of the Flies
Macbeth
Master Harold...
  And the Boys
MAUS
Medea
Merchant of Venice
Middlemarch
Middlesex
Mockingjay
Montana 1948
Mother Courage and
  Her Children
Mrs. Dalloway
My Antonia

My Brilliant Friend
My Children! My
  Africa!
Mythology
Never Let Me Go
Night
Oedipus Rex or
  Oedipus the King
Of Mice and Men
Oliver Twist
One Flew Over the
  Cuckoo's Nest
One Hundred Years
  of Solitude
O Pioneers
Oroonoko
Oryx and Crake
Othello
Our Town
Paper Towns
Percy Shelley:
  Poems

Persepolis: The
  Story of a
  Childhood
Poe's Poetry
Pride and Prejudice
Purple Hibiscus
Pygmalion
Reading Lolita in
  Tehran
Rhinoceros
Rip Van Winkle and
  Other Stories
Robert Frost: Poems
Robinson Crusoe
Roll of Thunder,
  Hear My Cry
Romeo and Juliet
Roots
Rosencrantz and
  Guildenstern Are
  Dead
Shakespeare's
  Sonnets

For our full list of over 300 Study Guides, Quizzes, Lesson Plans
Sample College Application Essays, Literature Essays and E-texts, visit:

www.gradesaver.com

Lesson Plans

GradeSaver™

Getting you the grade since 1999™

Other Lesson Plans from GradeSaver™

The Guest

The Handmaid's
Tale

The Heart Is a
Lonely Hunter

The Help

The History Boys

The Hobbit

The Homecoming

The Hot Zone

The Hound of the
Baskervilles

The House of
Bernarda Alba

The House of the
Spirits

The Hunger Games

The Importance of
Being Earnest

Their Eyes Were
Watching God

The Joy Luck Club

The Jungle

The Jungle Book

The Kite Runner

The Legend of
Sleepy Hollow

The Lone Ranger
and Tonto
Fistfight in
Heaven

The Long Goodbye

The Love Song of J.
Alfred Prufrock

The Martian
Chronicles

The Master and
Margarita

The Maze Runner

The Member of the
Wedding

The Metamorphosis

The Moonlit Road
and Other Ghost
and Horror
Stories

The Namesake

The Necklace

The Odyssey

The Old Man and
the Sea

The Once and
Future King

The Outsiders

The Overcoat

The Pearl

The Perks of Being
a Wallflower

The Phantom
Tollbooth

The Poisonwood
Bible

The Quiet American

The Red Badge of
Courage

The Rime of the
Ancient Mariner

The Road

The Scarlet Letter

Made in the USA
Coppell, TX
23 May 2020